'Let's not mince words. The [...] rich.' Max Gunther.

'The Zurich Axioms' is a term coined some years ago by a group of enterprising Swiss speculators in Wall Street who wanted to get rich, and refers to the remarkable, simple, innovative and extremely effective set of principles they evolved about the handling of investment and risk. The most inexperienced investor can use the Axioms successfully, provided he or she is willing to accept the basic premise that, in finance as in anything else, 'nothing venture, nothing gain' is a law against which there is no appeal. If you want to get rich, you must learn neither to avoid risk nor to court it foolhardily, but to *manage* it — and enjoy it, too.

The 12 major and 16 minor Axioms contained in this book are the codification of the group's hard thinking and experience: a practical philosophy of the realistic management of risk which can be followed by anyone, not merely the 'experts'. In fact, several of the Axioms fly right in the face of the traditional wisdom of the investment advice business — which may possibly explain why so many investors are not rich. But the Axioms do work. In forty years they have helped many people make a great deal of money, often from quite modest beginnings, while others acting in ignorance of them have frequently come to grief.

This book reveals these startlingly straightforward guidelines, enlivened by a wealth of case histories and wry commentary. It is not only extremely entertaining, but it will prove invaluable to any investor, whether in stocks, commodities, art, antiques or real estate, who is willing to take risk on its own terms and chance a little to gain a lot.

MAX GUNTHER was born in London of a British mother and a Swiss father. Just before the Second World War his family moved to New York, where his father became chairman of the New York branch of the Swiss Bank Corporation.

Max Gunther says, 'I always knew I wanted to write, but always knew too that writing is a slow way to try to make one's living. Hence I became interested in both writing (for fun) and speculating (for money) at the age of 10 or 11.' He made his first capital gain on the stock market at the age of 13, and sold his first written effort to a science fiction magazine at 15. Continuing as he started, he has written 24 books, including one novel, but 'by far the larger part of my income is from investment'.

Max Gunther is married to an American and has been a naturalised US citizen since 1953.

THE
ZURICH
AXIOMS

MAX GUNTHER

London
UNWIN PAPERBACKS
Boston   Sydney

First published in Great Britain by Souvenir Press Ltd in 1985
First published by Unwin Paperbacks in 1986

This book is copyright under the Berne Convention. No reproduction
without permission. All rights reserved.

UNWIN ® PAPERBACKS
40 Museum Street, London WC1A 1LU, UK

Unwin Paperbacks
Park Lane, Hemel Hempstead, Herts HP2 4TE, UK

Allen & Unwin Australia Pty Ltd
8 Napier Street, North Sydney, NSW 2060 Australia

Allen & Unwin with the Port Nicholson Press
PO Box 11−838 Wellington, New Zealand

Copyright © 1985 Max Gunther

CONDITION OF SALE: This book is sold subject to the condition that it
shall not, by way of trade or otherwise, be lent, re-sold, hired out or otherwise
circulated, without the publisher's prior consent in any form of binding
or cover other than that in which it is published and without a similar
condition including this condition being imposed on the purchaser.

PUBLISHER'S NOTE

This publication is designed to provide accurate and authoritative information with regard to the subject matter covered. It is sold with the
understanding that the publisher is not engaged in rendering legal,
accounting or other professional service. If legal advice or other expert
assistance is required, the service of a competent professional person should
be sought.

British Library Cataloguing in Publication Data

Gunther, Max
    The Zurich axioms.
1. Speculation
I. Title
332.64'5   HG6015
ISBN 0−04−332126−7

Printed and bound in Great Britain by Cox & Wyman Ltd, Reading

CONTENTS

CONTENTS

Introduction

What the Axioms Are and How They Came to Be

Consider the puzzle of Switzerland. This ancestral home of mine is a rocky little place about half the size of Maine. It has not one inch of seacoast. It is one of the most mineral-poor lands on earth. It possesses not a drop of oil to call its own, barely a bucket of coal. As for farming, its climate and topography are inhospitable to just about everything.

It has stayed out of European wars for 300 years, chiefly because, in all that time, there has never been an invader who really wanted it.

Yet the Swiss are among the most affluent people in the world. In per capita income they rank with the Americans, West Germans, and Japanese. Their currency is among the world's soundest.

How do the Swiss do it?

They do it by being the world's cleverest investors, speculators, and gamblers.

This book is about betting to win.

Perhaps that makes it sound like a book for everybody. It is not. Everybody wants to win, of course. But not everybody wants to bet, and therein lies a difference of the greatest magnitude.

Many people, probably most, want to win without betting. That is an entirely understandable wish. There is nothing reprehensible about it. Indeed, many of our hoariest old Work Ethic teachings urge it upon us. We are told that risk-taking is foolish. A prudent man or woman places no bets beyond those that are required by the unalterable basic terms of human existence. The well-lived life is a nose-to-the-grindstone life, perhaps somewhat dull but safe. A bird in the hand . . .

Well, everybody understands the trade-offs. If you have a philosophical bias against betting, you will find little that is useful to you in this book—unless, of course, it changes your mind.

But if you do not mind taking reasonable risks—or better, if you enjoy risk, as the Swiss do—then this book is for you. The Zurich Axioms are all about risk and its management. If you study the Axioms with the diligence they deserve, they can enable you to win more of your bets than you ever thought possible.

Let's not mince words. They can make you rich.

The book is about betting in its broadest sense. You will find the stock market mentioned frequently because that is where most of my experience has been, but the book is not limited to that great supermarket of dreams. The Axioms apply as well to speculation in commodities, precious metals, art or antiques; to gambles in real estate; to the thrust and parry of daily business; to casino and table gambling. The Axioms apply, in short, to any situation in which you put money at risk in order to get more money.

All of life is a gamble, as every adult knows. Many people, probably most, are unhappy with this fact and spend their lives figuring out how to place as few bets as possible. Others, however, take the opposite route, and among these are the Swiss.

Not all Swiss men and women display this trait, of course,

but large numbers do—enough, certainly, to allow for generalizations about the Swiss national character. The Swiss did not become the world's bankers by sitting in dark rooms chewing their fingernails. They did it by facing risk head-on and figuring out how to manage it.

The Swiss, amid their mountains, look around at the world and find it full of risk. They know it is possible to cut one's personal risks to a minimum—but they also know that if you do that, you abandon all hope of becoming anything but a face in the crowd.

To make any kind of gain in life—a gain of wealth, personal stature, whatever you define as "gain"—you must place some of your material and/or emotional capital at risk. You must make a commitment of money, time, love, *something*. That is the law of the universe. Except by blind chance, it cannot be circumvented. No creature on earth is excused from obedience to this pitiless law. To become a butterfly, a caterpillar must grow fat; and to grow fat, it must venture out where birds are. There are no appeals. It is the *law*.

The Swiss, observing all this, conclude that the sensible way to conduct one's life is not to shun risk but to expose oneself to it deliberately. To join the game; to *bet*. But not in the caterpillar's mindless way. To bet, instead, with care and thought. To bet in such a way that large gains are more likely than large losses. *To bet and win*.

Can this be done? Indeed. There is a formula for doing it. Or perhaps "formula" is the wrong word, since it suggests mechanical actions and a lack of choice. A better word might be "philosophy." This formula or philosophy consists of twelve profound and mysterious rules of risk-taking called the Zurich Axioms.

Be warned: The Axioms are somewhat startling when you first encounter them. They are not the kind of investment advice most counselors hand out. Indeed, they contradict some of the most cherished clichés of the investment-advice business.

The most successful Swiss speculators pay scant attention to conventional investment advice. They have a better way.

The term "Zurich Axioms" was coined by a club of Swiss stock and commodity plungers who collected around Wall Street after the Second World War. My father was one of the founding members. It wasn't a formal club. There were no by-laws, dues, or membership lists. It was simply a group of men and women who liked each other, wanted to get rich, and shared the belief that nobody ever got rich on a salary. They met irregularly at Oscar's Delmonico and other Wall Street watering places. The meetings continued all through the 1950s, 1960s, and 1970s.

They talked about many things, but mainly about risk. The work of codifying the Zurich Axioms got started when I asked my father a question he couldn't answer.

My father was a Swiss banker, Zurich-born and -bred. The given names on his birth certificate were Franz Heinrich, but in America everybody called him Frank Henry. When he died a few years ago his obituaries made much of the fact that he had headed the New York branch of the Schweizerbankver-ein—Zurich's financial colossus, the Swiss Bank Corporation. That job was important to him, but he once told me that what he really wanted engraved on his tombstone was this sentence: "He gambled and won."

Frank Henry and I started to talk about speculation while I was in high school. He would look at my report card and grumble that the curriculum was incomplete. "They don't teach you the thing you need most of all," he would say. "Speculation. How to take risks and win. A boy growing up in America without knowing how to speculate—why, that's like being in a gold mine without a shovel!"

And when I was in college and the army, trying to make choices about future careers, Frank Henry would say, "Don't just think in terms of a salary. People never get rich on salaries, and a lot of people get poor on them. You've got to have something else going for you. A couple of good speculations, that's what you need."

Typical Swiss talk. I absorbed it as part of my education. When I got out of the army with a few hundred dollars in back pay and poker winnings, I took Frank Henry's advice and shunned savings institutions, which he regarded with the greatest scorn. I put the money into the stock market. I won some, lost some, and ended with about the same amount I'd started with.

Meanwhile, Frank Henry was having a ball in the same market. Among other ventures, he made a bundle on some wildly speculative Canadian uranium-mining stocks.

"What *is* this?" I asked gloomily. "I invest prudently and get nowhere. You buy moose pasture and get rich. Is there something I don't understand?"

"You have to know how to do it," he said.

"Well, okay. Teach me."

He stared at me silently, stumped.

What he had in his head, it turned out, were rules of speculative play that he had absorbed over a lifetime. These rules are in the air—are understood but seldom articulated—in Swiss banking and speculative circles. Having lived in these circles since he got his first clerk-apprentice job at age seventeen, Frank Henry had assimilated the rules into his very bones. But he could not specifically identify them or explain them to me.

He asked his Swiss Wall Street friends about them. The friends didn't know exactly what the rules were either.

But from that moment on they made it their business to get the rules separated and clarified in their minds. It started as a game with them, but it grew more serious as the years went by.

They formed the habit of questioning themselves and one another about important speculative moves: "Why are you buying gold *now*? . . . What made you sell this stock when everybody else was buying? . . . Why are you doing *this* instead of *that*?" They forced each other to articulate the thinking that guided them.

The list of rules evolved gradually. It grew shorter, sharper, tidier, and more useful as time went on. Nobody remembers who coined the term "Zurich Axioms," but that is the name by which the rules came to be known and are still known.

The Axioms have not changed very much in the last several years. They have stopped evolving. As far as anybody knows, they are now in their final form: twelve Major Axioms and sixteen Minor Axioms.

Their value seems to me incalculable. They grow bigger each time I study them—a sure sign of fundamental verity. They are rich in secondary and tertiary layers of meaning, some coldly pragmatic, some verging on the mystical. They are not just a philosophy of speculation; they are guideposts for successful living.

They have made a lot of people rich.

The First Major Axiom:
ON RISK

Worry is not a sickness but a sign of health. If you are not worried, you are not risking enough.

Two young women friends graduated from college many years ago and decided to seek their fortunes together. They went to Wall Street and worked at a succession of jobs. Eventually both ended as employees of E. F. Hutton, one of the bigger stock brokerages. That was how they met Gerald M. Loeb.

Loeb, who died a few years ago, was one of the most respected investment counselors on the Street. This bald, genial man was a veteran of the hellish bear markets of the 1930s and the astounding bull markets that followed the Second World War. He kept his cool through all of it. He was born poor but died rich. His book *The Battle for Investment Survival* may have been the most popular market-strategy handbook of all time. It was certainly among the most readable, for Loeb was a born storyteller.

He told this story about the young women one night at a restaurant near the American Stock Exchange, where he had met Frank Henry and me for dinner. The story made a point he felt needed to be made about risk.

The young women both shyly approached him for investment advice. They approached him at separate times, but he knew of their close friendship and was certain they compared notes. Their financial situations in the beginning were identical. They had launched promising careers and were moving up modestly in pay and status. Their salary checks were beginning to do more than cover the bare essentials of existence. They had something left over after settling with the Internal Revenue Service each year. The amount was not large, but it was enough to be concerned about, and there was the promise of more in the future. Their question to Gerald Loeb: What should they do with it?

Over toast and tea at his favorite snack shop, the fatherly Loeb tried to sort out the trade-offs for them. But it quickly became apparent to him that each of them already had her mind made up. All they wanted from him was confirmation.

In telling the story, Loeb mischievously dubbed one of the women Sober Sylvia and the other Mad Mary. Sylvia's ambition for her money was to find a haven of perfect safety. She wanted to put the money into an interest-bearing bank account or some other savings-like deposit with an all-but-guaranteed return and all-but-guaranteed preservation of capital. Mary, on the other hand, wanted to take some risks in the hope of making her little handful of capital grow more meaningfully.

They carried out their respective strategies. A year later Sylvia had intact capital, an increment of interest, and a cozy feeling of security. Mary had a bloody nose. She had taken a beating in a stormy market. The value of her stocks had declined about 25 percent since she had bought them.

Sylvia was generous enough not to crow. Instead, she seemed horrified. "That's terrible!" she said when she learned the extent of her friend's misfortune. "Why, you've lost a quarter of your money. How awful!"

The three of them were having lunch together, as they occasionally did. Loeb watched Mary intently. He winced as he waited for her reaction to Sylvia's outburst of sympathy. He was afraid Mary's early loss would discourage her and drive her out of the game, as happens to many a neophyte speculator. ("They all expect to be big winners instantly," he would say mournfully. "When they don't triple their money the very first year they go off pouting like spoiled kids.")

But Mary had what it takes. She smiled, unperturbed. "Yes," she said, "it's true I've got a loss. But look what else I've got." She leaned across the table toward her friend. "Sylvia," she said, *I'm having an adventure."*

Most people grasp at security as though it were the most important thing in the world. Security does seem to have a lot going for it. It gives you that cozy immersed feeling, like being in a warm bed on a winter night. It engenders a sense of tranquillity.

Most psychiatrists and psychologists these days would consider that a good thing. It is the central assumption of modern psychology that mental health means, above all, being calm. This unexplored assumption has dominated shrinkish thought for decades. *How to Stop Worrying and Start Living* was one of the earlier books dealing with this dogma, and *The Relaxation Response* was one of the later ones. Worry is harmful, the shrinks assure us. They offer no trustworthy evidence that the statement is true. It has become accepted as true through sheer relentless assertion.

Devotees of mystical and meditational disciplines, particularly the eastern varieties, go still further. They value tranquillity so much that in many cases they are willing to endure poverty for its sake. Some Buddhist sects, for example, hold that one shouldn't strive for possessions and should even give away what one has. The theory is that the less you own, the less you will have to worry about.

The philosophy behind the Zurich Axioms is, of course, the exact opposite. Perhaps freedom from worry is nice in some ways. But any good Swiss speculator will tell you that if your main goal in life is to escape worry, you are going to stay poor.

You are also going to be bored silly.

Life ought to be an adventure, not a vegetation. An adventure may be defined as an episode in which you face some kind of jeopardy and try to overcome it. While facing the jeopardy, your natural and healthy response is going to be a state of worry.

Worry is an integral part of life's grandest enjoyments. Love affairs, for instance. If you are afraid to commit yourself and take personal risks, you will never fall in love. Your life may then be as calm as a tidal pool, but who wants it? Another example: sports. An athletic event is an episode in which athletes, and vicariously spectators, deliberately expose themselves to jeopardy—and do a powerful lot of worrying about it. It is a minor adventure for most of the spectators and a major one for the athletes. It is a situation of carefully created risk. We wouldn't attend sports events and other contests if we didn't get some basic satisfaction out of them. We need adventure.

Perhaps we need tranquillity at times too. But we get plenty of that at night when we sleep—plus, on most days, another couple of hours at odd times while we are awake. Eight or ten hours out of twenty-four ought to be enough.

Sigmund Freud understood the need for adventure. Though he was confused about the "purpose" of life and tended to lapse into incoherence when he strayed onto the topic, he did not harbor the unlikely belief that the purpose of life is to get calm. Many of his disciples did, but he didn't. Indeed, he went out of his way to poke fun at yoga and other eastern psycho-religious disciplines, which he regarded as the ultimate expression of the "get calm" school of mental-health teaching. In yoga, the object is to achieve inner peace at the expense of everything else. As Freud noted in *Civilization and Its Discontents,* anybody who fully achieves the goal of such a discipline "has sacrificed his life." And for what? "He has only achieved the happiness of quietness."

It seems like a bad bargain.

Adventure is what makes life worth living. And the way to have an adventure is to expose yourself to risk.

Gerald Loeb knew this. That was why he could not applaud Sober Sylvia's decision to put her money into a bank account.

Even when interest rates are relatively high, what is the payoff? At the beginning of the year you give a banker $100. At the end of the year he hands you back $109. Big deal. And what a dull business.

True, the safety of your $100 capital is just about guaranteed, at least in any reputable bank in the industrialized western world. Barring a major economic calamity, you aren't going to lose anything. The banker may lower the interest rate during the course of the year, but at least he won't hand you back any *less* than your original $100. But where is the fun? The fire? The passion? Where are the big brass bands?

And where is any hope of getting rich?

That $9 of interest is taxable as income. What's left after taxes will keep you even with inflation, perhaps. You won't make any appreciable change in your financial status that way.

Nor are you ever going to get rich on salary or wage income. It is impossible. The economic structure of the world is rigged against you. If you depend on job income as your main pillar of support, the best you can hope for is that you will get through life without having to beg for food. Not even that is guaranteed.

Oddly, the vast majority of men and women do depend principally on job income, with savings as a backup. It used to annoy Frank Henry that middle-class people in America are pushed in this direction inexorably by their education and social conditioning. "A kid can't escape it," he would grumble. "Teachers, parents, guidance counselors, and everybody else, they all keep hammering at the kid: 'Do your homework or you won't get a good job.' Getting a good job—that's supposed to be the high point of anybody's ambitions. But what about a good speculation? Why don't they talk to kids about that?"

I was one kid who got talked to about it plenty. Frank Henry's rule of thumb was that only half of one's financial energies should be devoted to job income. The other half ought to go into investment and speculation.

For here is the cold truth. Unless you have a wealthy relative, the only way you are ever going to lift yourself above the great unrich—*absolutely the only hope you have*—is to take a risk.

Yes, of course, it is a two-way street. Risk-taking implies the possibility of loss instead of gain. If you speculate with your money, you stand to lose it. Instead of ending rich, you can end poor.

But look at it this way. As an ordinary tax-hounded, inflation-raddled income-earner, carrying much of the rest of the world on your back, you are in a pretty sorry financial state anyhow. What real difference is it going to make if you get a bit poorer while trying to get richer?

You aren't likely to get much poorer, not with the Zurich Axioms as part of your equipment. But you *can* get very much richer. There is farther to go upward than downward—and no matter what happens, you will have an adventure. With the potential gain so much bigger than the potential loss, the game is rigged in your favor.

Gerald Loeb's two friends, Sylvia and Mary, illustrate what can happen. When I last had any news of them they were in their middle fifties. Both had been married and divorced, and both had continued to manage their financial affairs in the ways they had discussed with Loeb when they were starting out.

Sylvia had put all her spare cash into savings accounts, long-term certificates of deposit, local authority bonds, and other "safe" havens. The bonds were not as safe as she had been promised, for they all lost big percentages of their capital value during the wild and unexpected rise of general interest rates in the 1970s. Her bank accounts and CDs kept the rest of her capital intact, but the equally unexpected two-digit inflation of the 1970s eroded her money's spending power disastrously.

Her best move had been to buy a house when she was married. She and her husband were on the books as co-owners. When they divorced, they agreed to sell the house and split the equity fifty-fifty. The house had appreciated pleasantly in value during their years of ownership, so they walked away with considerably more money than they had put into it.

Still, Sylvia was not rich or anywhere near rich. She went back to work in a brokerage after her divorce and must continue to work until she becomes eligible for a pension in her sixties. The pension will not be much, but she cannot afford to abandon it, for her net wealth isn't big enough to carry her through her old age. She has designed her life so that job income is her main pillar of support. She probably will not starve, but she will always have to think hard before buying a new pair of shoes. She and her pet cats will live out their lives in a one-bedroom flat that never gets quite warm enough in the winter.

As for Mary, she got rich.

She was always concerned about safety of capital, as any sane person is, but she didn't let that one concern overwhelm all else in her financial philosophy. She took risks. After a painful start, she began to see some of the risks paying off. She did well in the buoyant stock market of the 1960s, but her most magnificent speculation was in gold.

The yellow metal first became available to American citizens as an investment medium in 1971, when President Nixon severed the official link between gold and the dollar. Until then the price had been pegged immovably at $35 per Troy ounce.

After the President's action, the price jumped. But Mary was quick. Against the advice of a lot of conservative counselors, she bought holdings in the metal at various prices in the range of $40 to $50.

Before the end of the decade, it hit $875. She sold most of her holdings at around $600. She had been comfortably well off before, but now she was rich.

She owns a house, a holiday cottage, and a piece of a Caribbean island. She spends much of her time traveling—and she travels first-class, of course. She quit her job long ago. As she explained to Gerald Loeb, job income had become a minor element in her financial picture. Her yearly take in stock dividends alone was more than her salary. It seemed disproportionate, therefore, to spend five of every seven days earning that salary.

It is true that Mary's financial affairs have given her a good deal of worry over the years, probably much more worry than Sylvia has ever known. Perhaps this will be some consolation to Sylvia in her unrich old age. Sylvia has never had to go to bed wondering if she would wake up rich or poor. She has always been able to make some kind of calculation about her financial condition next year or ten years hence. The calculation has not always been accurate, especially during the years when her bonds were melting like ice in the sun, but at least she could arrive at an approximation. That must have been comforting.

Mary, by contrast, was never able to do more than make wild guesses about her future during the years when she was acquiring her wealth. There were undoubtedly nights when she slept poorly or not at all. There were times when she was frightened.

But look what she got in return.

Many of Wall Street's most celebrated plungers have said publicly that a state of almost constant worry is a part of their way of life. Few of them say this by way of complaint. They are almost always cheerful about it. They *like* it.

One of the most exalted speculators was Jesse Livermore, who flourished on the Street during the early days of this century. A tall, handsome man with startling light-blond hair, Livermore drew crowds wherever he went. People were always asking him for investment advice, and he was continually hounded by newspaper and magazine reporters trying to pry bits of quotable wisdom out of him. An earnest young newsman went up to him one day and asked if he felt it was worthwhile to become a millionaire, considering all the strife and struggle one had to go through to get there. Livermore responded that he liked money a lot, so it was certainly worthwhile to him. But aren't there nights when a stock trader can't sleep? the reporter pursued. Is life worth living when you're worried all the time?

"Well, now, kid, I'll tell you," Livermore said. "Every occupation has its aches and pains. If you keep bees, you get stung. Me, I get worried. It's either that or stay poor. If I've got a choice between worried and poor, I'll take worried anytime."

Livermore, who made and lost four huge fortunes by speculating in stocks, not only accepted the state of worry but seemed to enjoy it. He and Frank Henry were having a couple of drinks in a bar one evening when Livermore suddenly remembered he was supposed to be at a dinner party. He phoned an embarrassed apology to the hostess, then ordered another drink and explained to Frank Henry that he tended to get distracted and forgetful whenever he was involved in a chancy move on the market. Frank Henry remarked that as far as he'd ever been able to observe, there was never a time when Livermore *wasn't* involved in a chancy move. Livermore agreed readily. If he wasn't actually in the middle of a move at any given time, he was worrying about half a dozen he might be making next week.

He admitted that he worried about his speculations all the time, even in his sleep. But then he said that was all right by him. "It's the way I want it," he said. "I don't think I'd enjoy life half as much if I always knew how rich I was going to be tomorrow."

Frank Henry remembered that and was still quoting it decades later. It expresses the philosophy of the First Axiom. Unfortunately, Jesse Livermore did not have all the other Axioms to help him, and his story did not end happily. We will come back to him later.

All this talk of risk and worry may make it sound as though the speculator's life is lived at the edge of a precipice. This isn't so. True, there are times when you get that shuddery feeling, but such times come rarely and don't usually last long. Most of the time you will be worried only enough to make life spicy. The degree of risk we are talking about really isn't very great.

Virtually all gain-oriented financial manipulation involves risk, whether one calls oneself a speculator or not. The only nearly risk-free course you can take with your money is to put it into an interest-bearing bank account, a government bond, or some other savings-like deposit. There is risk even in doing that. Banks are known to fail. If a bank collapsed with your money stuck inside it, the Federal Deposit Insurance Corporation (FDIC) would reimburse you, but only after a long delay and with no interest. If dozens of banks were to turn belly-up all at once in some nationwide economic catastrophe, then not even the FDIC would be able to fulfill its obligations. It, too, would fail. Nobody knows what would happen to depositors' money in a situation like that. Luckily, there is only a small chance that such nightmares will come to pass. A bank account is as close to riskless as any investment you are ever going to find in this chancy world.

Precisely because the risk is low, however, the return is low.

Seeking a better payoff, acquisitive men and women turn to other, riskier gambles with their money. Yet strangely, most do this without admitting they are doing it. They pretend they are being very prudent and sensible. They aren't taking risks. They aren't speculating, they aren't—whisper the dreaded word!— *gambling*. No, they're "investing."

The supposed difference between investing and speculating deserves to be explored, for it may have been getting in your way as you tried to come to grips with the First Axiom. We students of the Zurich Axioms frankly call ourselves speculators. This may make it sound to you as though you are being urged or will be urged to take wild and harebrained chances. You may think you'd rather be an investor than a speculator. Being an investor sounds safer.

In truth, however, there is no difference whatever. As the plain-talking Gerald Loeb put it, "All investment is speculation. The only difference is that some people admit it and some don't."

It's like the difference between luncheon and lunch. You get the same liverwurst sandwich either way. The only difference is in the impression somebody wants to make.

People who offer to counsel you in money management almost always call themselves "investment" advisers, not speculation advisers. It sounds more serious and impressive that way (and also makes for higher fees). Tip sheets, newsletters, and magazines serving the various speculative worlds nearly always call themselves "investment" publications. But they are all dealing with speculation just as the Zurich Axioms do. They just don't like to say it.

There is even a class of securities that financial experts like to call "investment-grade." That makes them sound very dignified, awe-inspiring, and super-safe. An adviser, talking about such a security in appropriately solemn tones, can convince a novice that this is the long-sought high-paying investment without risk.

Like IBM stock. IBM is the bluest of the blue chips. Its nickname around Wall Street is Big Blue. You're always safe buying an investment-grade security like IBM, right?

Sure. If you'd bought IBM at its peak price in 1973, when nearly every adviser in the world was touting it, you'd have had to wait nine years to get your money back. You would have been better off keeping your money in a sock.

There is no risk-free speculation, no matter how dignified it may sound. For another example, take General Motors. This stock, too, has usually appeared on brokerage lists of the great investment-grade securities. It was on all the lists back in 1971, when everybody thought GM was going to own the world. There was nothing speculative about it, they all said. It was the kind of stock that conservative estate executors bought for orphans. It was an *investment*.

But something went wrong with this wonderful investment-grade security. If you had bought it at its peak in 1971, you would *still* be waiting to get your money back.

Calling it an investment doesn't change the facts: A gamble is still a gamble. You'd think they would have learned this in the debacle of 1929, when all of Wall Street was suddenly revealed as nothing but a gigantic roulette wheel, gobbling up gamblers' money at a horrifying rate. The stories of 1929's great investment-grade stocks can make you weep. New York Central Railroad: $257 in 1929, down to $9 three years later. Radio Corporation, the ancestor of RCA: from $574 to $12. And a younger GM: from $1,075 to $40.

All investment is speculation, as Loeb said. You put up your money and you take your chances. You're a speculator whether you are betting on GM or anything else. You might as well admit it. There is no sense in trying to hoodwink yourself. You understand the world better when you come to it with your eyes wide open.

The Zurich Axioms are about speculation and say they are. It doesn't mean they are about goofy chance-taking. It means only that they are frank.

MINOR AXIOM I.
Always play for meaningful stakes.

"Only bet what you can afford to lose," says the old bromide. You hear it in Las Vegas, on Wall Street, and wherever people risk money to get more money. You read it in books of investment and money-management advice by conventional counselors like Sylvia Porter. It is repeated so often and in so many places that it has taken on an aura of truth through assertion— just like the shrinks' bromide about getting calm.

But you should study it with the greatest care before making it a part of your speculative toolkit. As most people interpret it, it is a formula that almost assures poor results.

What is an amount that you can "afford to lose"? Most would define it as "an amount which, if I lose it, won't hurt." Or "an amount which, if I lose it, won't make any significant difference in my general financial well-being."

A buck or two, in other words. Twenty bucks. A few hundred. These are the kinds of amounts most middle-class people would consider loss-affordable. And as a result, these are the kinds of amounts most middle-class people speculate with, if they speculate at all.

But consider this. If you bet $100 and double your money, you're still poor.

The only way to beat the system is to play for meaningful stakes. This doesn't mean you should bet amounts whose loss would bankrupt you. You've got to pay the rent and feed the kids, after all. But it does mean you must get over the fear of being hurt.

If an amount is so small that its loss won't make any significant difference, then it isn't likely to bring you any significant gains either. The only way to win a big payoff from a small wager is to go for a long, long shot. You might buy a $1 lottery ticket and win a million, for instance. That is nice to dream about, but the odds against you, of course, are depressingly high.

In the normal course of speculative play, you must start out with a willingness to be hurt, if only slightly. Bet amounts that worry you, if only a little.

Perhaps you will want to start out modestly and then increase the dosage of worry as you gain experience and confidence in your own tough psyche. Every speculator finds his or her own level of tolerable risk. Some, like Jesse Livermore, bet so boldly that they can go broke with spectacular speed—and as we've noted, Livermore did, four times. His risk level was so high that it scared other speculators, even veteran ones. Frank Henry used to study Livermore's gambles and come home shaking his head in stunned amazement. "The man is mad!" Frank Henry would say. His own risk level was lower. He estimated once that if all his speculations blew up in his face in a single great cataclysm, when the smoke cleared he would be worth roughly half of what he had been before.

He would lose 50 percent. On the other hand, he would keep 50 percent. That was his chosen degree of worry.

Another man who believed in playing for meaningful stakes was J. Paul Getty, the oil tycoon. His story is instructive. Most people seem to think he inherited his huge wealth from his father, or at least inherited the seeds of it. The facts are quite otherwise. J. Paul Getty made that monumental pile on his own, beginning as an ordinary middle-class speculator like you and me.

It irritated him beyond endurance that people thought he had had life handed to him on a silver platter. "Where does this notion *come* from?" he shouted at me once, exasperated. (I met him at *Playboy*. He was a stockholder in the magazine's parent company, served for some years as its business and finance editor, and wrote thirty-four articles for it. This was his way of relaxing when he wasn't tycooning.)

He finally concluded that the enormous size of his fortune was what made nearly everybody leap to a wrong assumption. People evidently found it too hard to believe that a man could start with a modest, middle-class kind of stake and make a *billion* on his own.

But that is exactly what Getty did. The only advantage he had over you and me was that he started early in this century, when everything cost less and there was no income tax. He got no money from his somewhat frosty and forbidding father beyond a couple of modest loans, which he was required to pay back on a no-excuses schedule. The most valuable thing he received from his father was not money but instruction.

The senior Getty, George F., was a Minneapolis lawyer and self-taught speculator who struck it rich in the Oklahoma oil boom at the start of the century, developing rules of play that sound a little like some of the Zurich Axioms. He was a man with stern, unbending beliefs rooted in the Work Ethic. As J. Paul wrote in *Playboy*, "George F. rejected any ideas that a successful man's son should be pampered or spoiled or given money as a gift after he was old enough to earn his own living." And so young J. Paul struck out to seek his fortune on his own.

He had originally thought he wanted to join the diplomatic corps or become a writer, but his father's love of speculation was in his blood. He was drawn to Oklahoma and oil. Working as a roustabout and tooldresser, he accumulated a few hundred dollars. As his little pile grew, so did the urge to put it at risk.

It was now that he displayed his understanding of the principle underlying Minor Axiom i. He had learned this principle from his father. *Always play for meaningful stakes.*

He could have bought a piece of the action for $50 or even less. There was no shortage of opportunities to do this. The oilfields swarmed with wildcatters and speculative syndicates that needed money to continue drilling. They would sell tiny shares to anybody with a few bucks. But Getty knew he would never get rich on tiny shares.

Instead he went after something bigger. Near the little hamlet of Stone Bluff, another speculator was offering a half share in an oil lease that looked promising to Getty. He decided to bet on it. He bid $500, nearly his entire wad. Nobody topped his bid, and J. Paul Getty was officially in the oil business.

In January 1916, the first test well on the lease hit pay dirt: more than 700 barrels of crude oil a day. Not much later, Getty sold his interest for $12,000, and that was how his fabled fortune was founded.

"Of course, I was lucky," he said many years later, looking back on that seminal adventure of long ago. "I could have lost. But even if I had, that wouldn't have changed my conviction that I was right to take the chance. By taking a chance—a pretty big chance, I'll admit—I gave myself the possibility of getting somewhere interesting. The possibility, the *hope*, you see. If I'd refused to take the chance, I would not have had the hope."

He added that even if he had lost, it would not have been the end of his world. He would simply have scrabbled some more money together and tried again. "So it seemed to me I had a lot more to win than lose," he reminisced. "If I won, it would be various kinds of wonderful. If I lost, it would hurt, but not all that much. The right course of action seemed clear. What would you have done?"

MINOR AXIOM II.
Resist the allure of diversification.

Throughout the length and breadth of the investment world, they call it diversification. They could just as easily call it diversity.

That's an indication of how overblown it is.

After all these decades of usage it's too late to change the word now, so I will go on using it in the commonly accepted way. Diversification. Let's see what this ponderous and inelegant word means and how it might affect you in your efforts to grow rich.

As used in the investment community, it means spreading your money around. Spreading it thin. Putting it into a lot of little speculations instead of a few big ones.

The idea is safety. If six of your investments get nowhere, maybe six others will get somewhere. If Hey Wow Electronics goes bankrupt and the value of your stock drops to 3 cents, maybe your Hoo Boy Computer speculation will turn out better. If everything collapses, maybe your bonds, at least, will increase in value and keep you afloat.

That is the rationale. In the litany of conventional investment advice, having a "diversified portfolio" is among the most revered of all financial goals. Only one thing tops it: having a diversified portfolio of investment-grade securities. If you've got that, you've got the world by the tail!

Or so they like to tell you. The fact is that diversification, while reducing your risks, reduces by the same degree any hope you may have of getting rich.

Most of us middle-class plungers, at the start of our speculative adventures, have only a limited amount of capital to play with. Let's say you have $5,000. You want to make it grow. What are you going to do with it? The conventional wisdom would say diversify. Make ten bets of $500 each. Buy $500 worth of GM because the auto industry looks lively, put $500 into a savings account in case interest rates go up, $500 into gold in case the bottom drops out of everything, and so on. There—you're covered for all kinds of eventualities. Makes you feel safe, doesn't it? Safe from just about everything— including the danger of getting wealthy.

Diversification has three major flaws:

1. It forces you to violate the precept of Minor Axiom i: that you should always play for meaningful stakes. If your entire starting capital is itself not very meaningful, diversifying is only going to make things worse. The more you diversify, the smaller your speculations get. Carry it to extremes and you can end with amounts that are really quite trivial.

As we observed under Minor Axiom i, a hefty gain on a small amount leaves you just about where you started: still poor. Let's say your $500 speculation on Hoo Boy Computer works brightly, and the stock price doubles. What's your gain? Five hundred bucks. You are never going to get into the upper tax brackets that way.

2. By diversifying, you create a situation in which gains and losses are likely to cancel each other out, leaving you exactly where you began—at Point Zero.

You bought two stocks which were, we'll say, of somewhat less than investment grade: Hoo Boy Computer and Hey Wow Electronics. If the two companies were to be blessed with boom conditions, you figured, the trading prices of their stocks would rise. All right, let's say your hunch was correct. The companies have prospered, and you've gained $200 on each of those $500 speculations.

But at the time you were buying Hoo Boy and Hey Wow, your investment adviser solemnly warned you to hedge your bets by diversifying. In case of bad times, he said, you ought to get into some fixed–interest stock and gold.

So you bought $500 worth of gold and $500 worth of fixed–interest stock. And now here you are in the middle of a boom. Interest rates are soaring because of business and consumer loan demand, so the value of your fixed–interest stock is sagging. It's gone down $100. As for gold, everybody who owns the yellow metal is frantically selling it to raise cash. They all want to get into the thundering Wall Street bull market or put their money into those tempting new bank accounts with the eye-bugging interest rates. The value is leaking out of your gold like water out of an old rusty bucket. It's down $300.

So you have gained $400 on Hoo Boy and Hey Wow but lost $400 on your fixed–interest stock and gold. The whole exercise has been a waste of time and effort. What's the use?

3. By diversifying, you become a juggler trying to keep too many balls in the air all at once.

If you have just a few speculations going and one or two turn sour, you can take defensive action. The Third Axiom and others will address this situation. But if you have a dozen balls in the air and half of them start to go in the wrong direction, your chances of getting out of the dilemma without a black eye are not very good.

The more speculations you get into, the more time and study they will require. You can become hopelessly confused. When things go wrong—which is inevitable, as you are surely aware —you can be driven to near-panic as one problem after another presents itself. What often happens to people in this kind of pickle, especially novice speculators, is that they become paralyzed. They fail to take any action at all because they are being pressured to make too many painful decisions too fast. They can only stand and gape, stunned, as their wealth dwindles away.

When you think about these three major flaws of diversification and weigh them against its single advantage, safety, it begins not to look so good.

A little diversity probably won't do any harm. Three good speculations, maybe four, maybe even six if you are strongly attracted to that many all at once. My personal rule of thumb is to have no more than four going at any one time, and most often I keep the number to three or less—sometimes just one. I'm uncomfortable with more. This is largely a matter of personal preference and individual thinking habits. If you feel you can effectively handle a higher number, go for it.

But don't diversify just for the sake of diversity. You then become like a contestant in a supermarket shopping contest, in which the object is to fill your basket fast. You go home with a lot of expensive junk you don't really want. In speculation, you should put your money into ventures that genuinely attract you, *and only those*. Never buy something simply because you think you need it to round out a "diversified portfolio."

As some say around Wall Street, "Put all your eggs in one basket, and then watch the basket." This is one old financial bromide that stands scrutiny. Whoever first said it was obviously not a diversification fan. It is much easier to watch one or a few baskets than a dozen. When the fox comes around to steal your eggs, you can handle him without whirling around in circles.

Speculative Strategy

Now let's review the First Axiom quickly. Specifically, what does the axiom advise you to do with your money?

It says put your money at risk. Don't be afraid of getting hurt a little. The degree of risk you will usually be dealing with is not hair-raisingly high. By being willing to face it, you give yourself the only realistic chance you have of rising above the great unrich.

The price you pay for this glorious chance is a state of worry. But this worry, the First Axiom insists, is not the sickness modern psychology believes it to be. It is the hot and tart sauce of life. Once you get used to it, you enjoy it.

The Second Major Axiom:
ON GREED

Always take your profit too soon.

Amateurs on Wall Street do it. Amateurs in poker games do it. Amateurs everywhere do it. They stay too long and lose.

What makes them do it is greed, and that is what the Second Axiom is about. If you can conquer greed, that one act of self-control will make you a better speculator than 99 percent of other men and women who are scrambling after wealth.

But it is a hard act to pull off successfully. Greed is built into the human psyche. Most of us have it in big amounts. It has probably inspired more Sunday sermons than any other of our less than laudable traits. The sermons tend to have a despairing sound, with sighs for periods. The despair stems from the feeling that greed is so deeply entrenched in our souls that we can no more easily extract it than change the color of our eyes.

Patently, it cannot be exorcised by sermons. Sermons have never had the slightest effect against it. You are not likely to conquer it either by listening to other people's sermons or by preaching at yourself. A more pragmatic and promising course would be to think about the rich, strange paradox that lies at the heart of the Second Axiom: by reducing your greed, you improve your chances of getting rich.

Let's pause to define our terms. Greed, in the context of the

---

Second Axiom, means excessive acquisitiveness: wanting more, more, always more. It means wanting more than you came in for or more than you have a right to expect. It means losing control of your desire.

Greed is the bloated, self-destructive cousin of acquisitiveness. As we use the term here, "acquisitiveness" is the natural wish to improve one's material well-being. The Zurich Axioms were put together by people with a healthy dose of acquisitiveness, and it is unlikely you would be studying the Axioms unless you, too, had the trait. Every animal on earth has the instinct to acquire food, a nesting place, and the means of self-protection, and in this respect we differ from other creatures only in that our wants are more complicated. Don't be ashamed of being an acquirer. The trait is part of your survival equipment.

But acquisitiveness gone haywire, acquisitiveness gone out of control to the extent that it defeats its own purposes—that is greed. Fear and hate it. It is a speculator's enemy.

One man who made a nearly lifelong study of greed was Sherlock Feldman, for many years casino manager of the Dunes, one of the bigger Las Vegas gambling clubs. A beefy man with thick-rimmed glasses and a look of sad good humor, Feldman used to observe his club's patrons during his chosen duty hours of 2:00 a.m. to 10:00 a.m. daily, and what he saw often made him break into fits of philosophy.

"If they wanted less, they'd go home with more," he would say. That was his own axiom on greed.

He understood greed well, for he was himself an accomplished gambler. He made and lost several small fortunes in his youth but finally learned to control himself and died comfortably rich. Talking about his patrons at the Dunes, he would say, "What they do in here doesn't matter all that much for most of them. They're just playing. They lose a couple of hundred, who cares? But if the way they play here is the way they play their lives, then maybe it matters. You can tell why they aren't rich, a lot of them. Just watching them in here, you can see why they'll never get anyplace that counts."

He told of a woman who came in with a little wad of money that she was prepared to lose for fun. "She goes to a roulette wheel and puts $10 on one number. I forget what it was, her lucky number or birthdate or something. And what do you know? The number comes up, and she's richer by $350. So she takes $100 and puts it on some other number, and *that* number comes up! She collects three and a half big ones this time. All her friends gather round and tell her to bet some more, this is her lucky night. She looks at them, and I can see her starting to get greedy."

Feldman paused in telling the story to mop his forehead with a handkerchief. "Well, she goes on betting. She's had enough long shots, so she starts betting on the colors and the dozens —bets a few hundred each time and goes on winning. Six, seven wins in a row. She's really on a streak, this woman! Finally she has something like $9,800. You'd think that would be enough, right? I'd have stopped long before. A couple of grand would have made me happy. But this woman isn't even happy with $9,800. She's dizzy with greed by now, see. She keeps saying she only needs another couple of hundred to make ten grand."

Reaching for that big round number, she began to lose. Her capital dwindled. She placed bigger bets at greater odds to recoup it. Finally she lost everything, including her original $10.

This story illustrates the original meaning of the popular admonition "Don't push your luck"—or, as the Swiss more often put it, "Don't stretch your luck." Most people use it in casual speech without understanding that it has a serious meaning. It deserves more careful study than it usually gets.

What it means is this. In the course of gambling or speculative play, you will from time to time enjoy streaks and runs of luck. You will enjoy them so much that you will want to ride them for ever and ever. Undoubtedly you will have the good sense to recognize that they cannot last forever, but if greed has you in its grip, you will talk yourself into hoping or believing that they will at least last a long time . . . and then a bit longer . . . and then just a *little* longer. And so you will ride and ride, and in the end you and your money will go over the falls.

We will study the troublesome phenomenon of winning streaks in more detail when we come to the Fifth Axiom. (The Axioms are intricately interwoven. It is hardly possible to talk about one without mentioning others.) For now, the point to be appreciated is that you cannot know in advance how long a given winning streak is going to last. It *might* last a long time. On the other hand, it might end with the next tick of the clock.

What should you do, then? You should assume that any set or series of events producing a gain for you will be of short duration, and that your profit, therefore, won't be extravagantly big.

Yes, certainly, that lovely set of events might continue until it produces a colossal win. *Might.* But from where you stand at the beginning of the set, needing to make a sit-or-quit decision without being able to see the future, you are much better off playing the averages. The averages overwhelmingly favor quitting early. Long, high winning streaks make news and get talked about at parties, but they are newsworthy for the very reason that they are rare. Short, modest ones are vastly more common.

Always bet on the short and modest. Don't let greed get you. When you have a good profit, cash out and walk away.

Once in a while you will regret having walked away. The winning set will continue without you, and you will be left morosely counting all the money you didn't make. In hindsight, your decision to quit will look wrong. This depressing experience happens to every speculator once in a while, and I won't try to minimize it. It can make you want to cry.

But cheer up. To match against the time or two when the decision to quit early turns out wrong, there will be a dozen or two dozen times when it turns out right. In the long run, you make more money when you control your greed.

Always take your profit too soon, the Second Axiom says. Why "too soon"? What does that puzzling little phrase mean? It refers to the need to cash out before a set of winning events has reached its peak. Don't ever try to squeeze the last possible dollar from a set. It seldom works. Don't worry about the possibility that the set still has a long way to go—the possibility of regret. Don't *fear* regret. Since you can't see the peak, you must assume it is close rather than far. Take your profit and get out.

It is like climbing a mountain on a black, foggy night. The visibility is zero. Up above you and ahead of you somewhere is the peak, and on the other side is a sheer drop to disaster. You want to climb as high as you can. Ideally, you would like to reach the peak and stop exactly there. But you know "ideally" doesn't happen often in real life, and you aren't naive enough to think it is going to happen now. So the only sensible course is to stop climbing when you have reached what you consider a good height. Stop short of the peak. Stop *too soon*.

Sure, when the fog clears and the sun comes up, you may find you're less than halfway to the top. You could have climbed a lot farther. But don't nurse this regret. You aren't all the way up, but you *are* up. You've made a solid gain. What's more, you've made it and kept it. You are a good deal better off than all the blunderers who scrambled blindly to the peak and toppled over the other side.

This happened to a lot of real estate speculators in the early 1980s. As an example, consider the sad story of Alice and Harry, a Connecticut couple. They told me about their experience because they felt they had learned much from it. That which hurts, teaches. They wanted to explore their new knowledge. I promised not to reveal their identities. Alice and Harry are not their real names.

They are a married couple in their mid-forties, both of them attractive, bright, and acquisitive. Both hold jobs that pay good salaries. Their combined incomes, life-style, and general social orientation place them somewhere at the lower edge of the upper middle class. They have two kids in college.

Like many middle-income people in this end of the twentieth century, they have always found it a struggle to live within their income. They have not been able to put much aside for investment, and what they have invested has gone mainly into bank accounts, life insurance, and other savings-like deposits. Their one good speculation has been their family home.

In the early 1970s they went to Connecticut's affluent Fairfield County and bought a house that stretched their financial capabilities to the limit. This was a deliberate decision. After saving for years and still feeling unrich, they were beginning to develop an awareness of the First Axiom. They were coming to understand that they hadn't been risking enough.

As many middle-class people do, they looked at their home as a double-duty entity: not only a place to live but also a way to score a capital gain, maybe a big one. The speculation turned out to be an excellent one. Real estate values in Fairfield County rose spectacularly in the 1970s (though not as spectacularly as in some other places like California's Marin County or Florida's Dade). Early in the 1980s, Harry and Alice, estimating conservatively, figured that the market value of their home was something like two and a half to three times what they had paid for it less than a decade before.

It was time to sell. The kids were grown and gone. Alice and Harry didn't need a big house anymore. Indeed, both were fed up with suburban life and the burdens of homeownership. They wanted to move into a smaller, easier place, perhaps a rental apartment. The healthy growth in their home's capital value made the idea of selling look still more attractive. They had a dandy gain. The market value of their home had multiplied threefold or so, but because of the leverage supplied by their mortgage loan—an effect exactly like that of buying stocks or commodity futures on margin—they had more than sixfolded the value of their own capital invested in the venture. Not a bad showing at all.

But greed got them. They held on for more.

Alice recalls that they had read or heard about people in places like Marin County whose homes' market value had tenfolded in ten years. "We thought, wouldn't that be lovely?" she says. "We thought, if it can happen in Marin, then it can happen in Fairfield. If our house tenfolded, we'd be millionaires!"

Harry recalls that his main motivation was the fear of regret. "I said to myself, well, sure, it's nice that we can sell this place for three times what we paid. But suppose we sell it, and then suppose a few years down the pike, I find out that the guy I sold it to turned around and resold it for triple what *he* paid. I'll kick myself!"

So they held on. Reached the peak. And fell into the canyon on the other side.

As happens much more often than not, the peak was far closer than they wanted to believe. The real estate market in Fairfield—as in most of the suburban United States—collapsed in 1981 and 1982, particularly the market for big houses. In some neighborhoods, houses could hardly be sold at any price. When Alice and Harry belatedly put their house on the market, the world rudely declined to beat a path to their door. There were few lookers and even fewer serious shoppers. Even the local realtors, normally an ebullient lot, seemed bored and discouraged. In a whole year on the market, Alice and Harry received just one offer from a buyer. The amount offered was shockingly low. It was more than they had paid for the house, but not by much. They would have earned more by keeping their capital in a savings account.

When I last saw them they were waiting for the slumped market to recover. They had learned. They were not hoping any longer to make a killing on their house. They had arrived at an idea of the price at which they would like to sell it—a price that gave them a good profit but not a bonanza. They were determined to sell whenever they could get that price, no matter how buoyant the market or how high everybody's expectations for the future.

They were determined, in other words, to sell too soon. I hope they stick with that decision.

Carrying out the precept of the Second Axiom seems to be extraordinarily difficult for some. The main difficulty may be the fear of regret. This fear was Harry's worst enemy and may continue to be. Harry is not alone.

The fear is particularly common and particularly intense around the stock market. "Never check the price of a stock you've sold," says one of Wall Street's ancient teachings. The admonition isn't designed to help you make money but simply to protect you from weeping fits. The "left-behind blues," as Streeters call the malady, is felt to be among the most painful of all ailments stock speculators must contend with.

Painful? Oh Lord, yes. Like the time I sold Gulf Oil at about $31 and watched it soar to nearly $60 a year later. Or the time I dumped 1,500 shares of IBM at $70 and a fraction, and the doggone stock then leaped to $130. Or the time . . . but enough, enough! One must try not to torture oneself. Instead of glooming over these outcomes, I should be congratulating myself on all the times when selling too soon was brilliantly correct.

I *should* be, but even for one as thoroughly steeped in the Axioms as myself, the blues come creeping in the night. I promised you that I wouldn't minimize the pain of possible regret, and I won't. It can indeed hurt. I have no medicines to offer. There is no analgesic for this pain. It is simply something every speculator must put up with.

The fear of regret may be bad around Wall Street because the trading prices of stocks are quoted every business day. This is true of some other speculative media but not of others—not of real estate, for instance. You may have a broad, vague idea of the long-term ups and downs in the market value of your home, or holiday cottage in the Caribbean, but you can't get a precise fix on it every day in the *Wall Street Journal*. This lack of daily quotes provides you with some emotional protection. It buffers you. Unless the place is actually on the market and you are hearing offers, you can't do much more than guess what price it might bring. You are similarly and blessedly uninformed about the market value of a home you sold last year or ten years ago.

But if you speculate in stocks, you can pick up the paper any day, or phone your broker, and find out to the penny what people were willing to pay yesterday for any actively traded stock you own, ever owned, or ever wanted to own. A month or a year after you've cashed out, you can, if you wish, torment yourself by looking to see if the winning set continued without you.

Stock speculators are always doing that and are always working themselves into frenzies over it. Such a frenzy can cloud one's judgment to a hazardous degree.

I had a drink one night with an old friend of Frank Henry's, a South American speculator. He was feeling sorry for himself and seemed to have been drinking all afternoon. His story came out in pieces. When I finally was able to fit them together, I saw that I had been listening to a financial tragedy.

It had always been Frank Henry's opinion that this likable man was too emotional for the Wall Street game. I didn't know about that, though I did know the man was always getting his pockets emptied by Americans and Swiss who liked to lure him into high-stakes poker games. As he poured out the pieces of his sad story, I began to think Frank Henry might have been right. The man had problems in the stock market for the same reason, probably, that he had problems at the poker table. The reason was that though he was intellectually aware of the right thing to do in various situations, he couldn't always steel himself to do it.

The particular problem that was troubling him that night had begun a long way back. He had bought a large bundle of stock in Wometco Enterprises, a company with interests in the TV and movie industries. The price rose pleasantly, then faltered. He had a good profit, and he saw no compelling reason to think the winning set had a lot farther to go. So, sensibly, he sold out. Whereupon, because of unforeseen events, the price quadrupled.

This threw him into a frenzy of rage and regret. It got so bad that he became afraid to sell *anything*. He was clutched by the fear that history would inexorably repeat itself—as soon as he sold a stock, *zoom*, up it would go. The fear seemed to have paralyzed him.

There were trades he knew he should be making, but he couldn't move. One situation in particular was tormenting him. After cashing out of Wometco he had put most of that money into another TV-movie company, Warner Communications. He had a solid understanding of the entertainment industry and, with better control, might have done well in it. His Warner stock rose, once again giving him a good profit. The combined Wometco-Warner parlay had just about doubled his money.

Enough, one might think. It was time to get out. As the Axiom puts it, it was *too soon*.

But he couldn't make the move. He held on to the stock.

And without warning, Warner's Atari video-games division tumbled into a quagmire of problems. Warner Communications stock lost about two-thirds of its value in one dizzy, non-stop plunge.

MINOR AXIOM III.
Decide in advance what gain you want from a venture, and when you get it, get out.

The purpose of Minor Axiom iii is to help you answer the always difficult and often paralyzing question *What is enough?*

As we've seen, greed is the main reason why this question is so hard to answer. However much one has, one wants more. That is the way humans are made.

But there is another factor that contributes heavily to the difficulty for many people, perhaps for nearly all. This is the peculiar fact that as a speculation succeeds and your wealth grows, every new position feels like a starting position.

You start out with $1,000, let's say. You put it into a margined bet on the price of silver. Your hunch is correct, and a year later you've got $2,000. You've doubled your money.

That's nice. If you could do that every year, you'd soon be a millionaire. But the baffling fact is that it doesn't *feel* as nice as it is. Instead, that money quickly comes to feel as though it is yours by some kind of entitlement. You tend to take it for granted, especially if it came to you rather slowly through the year rather than all at once. Instead of saying, "Hey, wow, I've doubled my money!" or "Hey, look at this, I've got a grand I didn't have before!" you feel as though you have always had this much wealth.

Your two grand doesn't feel like an ending position. It feels like a new starting position. Because of that, you are going to have a hard time extricating yourself from the venture.

This may seem puzzling to you if you haven't often speculated or at least played penny-ante poker. It may seem like a weird little problem that afflicts others but won't happen to you. It is understandable that you should think that, but you are being too optimistic. The problem afflicts almost everybody in time. There is only the most remote chance that you are immune. You must learn to deal with the problem when it hits you.

There are many kinds of human endeavors in which starting and ending positions are clearly seen, felt, and understood. Athletics, for instance. When a runner comes to the end of a mile race, he or she *knows* it's the end. There is no question of racing on for another mile in the hope of winning two gold medals instead of one. All energies are exhausted. The tape is broken; the winners are on the record books. It's all over. It is time to quit, rest, gather new energies for another day.

Few such clear break points exist in the world of gambling and speculation. Poker games end, it is true. Racetracks close at the end of the day. Once in a great while, a stock market venture of yours might end when a company in which you've invested is absorbed by a bigger company and passes out of existence. But most of the time you will be required to call your own endings.

This is very, very hard to do, so hard that most people fail to get the hang of it. (Most, indeed, fail even to grasp the necessity of it.) But it is a technique you must master. It is an essential part of a good speculator's equipment.

An ending is a time when you withdraw, breathe a sigh of relief, and briefly relax. Like a runner at the end of a race, you flop down on the grass at the side of the track. You think, "Okay, it's over. I've done what I set out to do. I've won my medal. I'll sit here a while and enjoy it." Or you think, "Well, all right, I lost, but it's ended. I'll rest, and think, and plan.

And tomorrow I'll race again." Either way, you have come to an ending.

But how do you arrive at such a clearly seen stopping place in a world where there are no finish-line tapes, no end-of-the-round bells? Especially when each succeeding position feels like a new starting position?

You've bought a handful of Union Carbide stock, let's say. Or you've invested in gold. Or you own a house. These are races that aren't going to "finish" in any ordinary future that you can foresee. Such a race is open-ended. No arbitrarily chosen measure of time or distance, no judge or referee will tell you when you can stop striving and flop down on the grass. You are required to do that yourself—you alone. *The race ends when you say it ends.*

Minor Axiom iii tells you how to arrive at this ending. Decide where the finish line is before you start the race.

Does this make it easy to cash out? No, of course not. But it does make the exercise much easier than to enter each speculation with the idea that it is a race with no ending.

Let's go back to the example we talked about before. You have $1,000 and you're attracted to a speculation in silver. Say to yourself, "I'm going into this with the purpose of . . ." (whatever the purpose may be). Don't make it grandiose. Keep it relatively modest. Doubling to $2,000 within two years, perhaps. Or increasing to $1,500 within one year. That is the finish line. Keep it in sight all the way through the race. And when you get there, quit.

Now see how this helps you psychologically. Here you are at the starting line with $1,000, looking forward to a time when it may grow to $2,000. You are not in a position to take the $2,000 for granted, for you don't have it yet and, as you are surely aware, may never get it. At this point in the venture, at the starting line, the hoped-for $2,000 feels like a prize worth striving for. It doesn't feel like a new starting position. It feels like an ending.

Keep this feeling alive in you as the venture matures. Nurture it. If and when you do reach your goal, unless there are truly compelling reasons to turn the ending position into a new starting position, keep faith with yourself and get out.

What might these "truly compelling reasons" be—the reasons for staying in a race that you had planned to end? Such reasons can arise only from a dramatic, unforeseen change in the events and circumstances surrounding your venture. Not merely a shift but an upheaval. A whole new situation has arisen, and this situation makes you not just hopeful but next to certain that the winning set will continue.

For example, suppose you're speculating in commodities. You've got some frozen-orange-juice futures. You've reached an ending position. Keeping faith with yourself, you're about to sell out and bank your profit. But then you hear that a freak freezing spell has destroyed a lot of the Florida citrus crop. In circumstances like that, it might be wise at least to stay in the race a while and see what happens.

But such situations are rare. Most of the time, arrival at an ending position should signal just one thing: It's over.

One excellent way to reinforce the "ending" feeling is to rig up some kind of reward for yourself. A medal, if you will. Promise yourself in advance that if and when you achieve your stated goal, you'll take some of the winnings and buy yourself a new car or coat, or a five-string banjo, or whatever makes you happy. Or you'll take your spouse or a friend out for a ridiculously expensive meal in the ritziest restaurant in town.

The ending thus becomes associated with an actual event, something concrete to look forward to. Many speculators use this psychological strategy on themselves, even when they are veterans of the game. Frank Henry used to reward himself with oysters and American-style steaks, which he loved and which weren't easy to find in his native Switzerland. Jesse Livermore, who sometimes had great difficulty bringing his speculations to a close, would reward himself for a win by buying a new item for his collection of antique shaving mugs. With Gerald Loeb's friend Mary, it was usually a new dress or suit.

Such rewards may seem trivial when compared with the amounts of money being wagered—in Livermore's case, sometimes seven-figure amounts—but what is important is the sense of *ending* that even a seemingly silly reward may engender. If it works for you, treasure it.

There are many investment counselors who would frown on this procedure. Ever since the eighteenth century, for reasons that nobody has ever been able to explain very well, there has been a widely held belief that investment money should be considered inviolable. You aren't supposed to spend it, especially for something frivolous like a plate of oysters or a new coat. There is a special phrase for such a sacrilegious act. It's called *invading capital*. The shame of it!

But as Gerald Loeb was fond of asking, "Why do you go to all the trouble of making this money? What's it there for? To look at?" Loeb was possibly the first counselor to say publicly, without apparent shame, that an investor/speculator should spend some of his or her winnings. Indeed, Loeb went so far as to urge spending a portion of one's gain in any gainful year, whether or not one has arrived at an ending position.

Investment capital is money just like any other money, Loeb pointed out. It needn't be segregated and marked "hands off." Certainly, there are all sorts of good reasons for sitting on it. It will comfort you in your old age, it's a parachute for emergencies, it's something to pass on to your kids, it gives you that cozy immersed feeling, and so on. All that is nice. But you might as well have a little fun with the money too. Skimming some off the top once in a while, especially at ending positions, is a better idea than it is generally credited with being.

For this reason, I would advise you to keep your speculative capital in some easily accessible form if you can. This is more readily accomplished in some speculative media than in others, of course. If your money is locked up in a house or a rare-coin collection, it may have to stay locked until you find a buyer. But more and more banks are offering flexible equity-access deals for nonliquid wealth of that kind. In effect, such a deal lets you get at your equity by borrowing against it at low rates of interest. Perhaps you can work out something like that.

In other speculative media the goal of ready access is easier to achieve and is getting still easier all the time. Banks and brokers handling stocks, stock options, commodities, currencies, and precious metals have developed highly innovative new kinds of accounts for their customers in recent years. I now keep all my stock market money in an odd-shaped basket called a cash management account, devised by my broker, Merrill Lynch. It is a combination of many things: partly an ordinary margin account through which I buy and sell stocks in the traditional way, partly a checking account, partly a Visa credit-card account. When dividends are paid out by stocks I own, the cash automatically lands in this hybrid account. If I don't use the money, it gets scooped into a deposit account. Anytime I want some of it, all I do is write a check or flash my Visa card. Checks and card charges are paid directly out of the account. That's what I call ready access.

It's a perfect setup for celebrating ending positions. When I hit such a position, my wife and my Visa card and I go off for a weekend of sinful luxury in New York.

Speculative Strategy

Now let's see just what the Second Axiom advises you to do.

It says, "Sell too soon." Don't wait for booms to reach their peaks. Don't hope for winning streaks to go on and on. Don't stretch your luck. Expect winning streaks to be short. When you reach a previously decided-upon ending position, cash out and walk away. Do this even when everything looks rosy, even when you're optimistic, even when everybody around you is saying the boom will keep roaring along.

The only reason for not doing it would be that some new situation has arisen, and this situation makes you all but certain that you can go on winning for a while.

Except in such unusual circumstances, get in the habit of selling too soon. And when you've sold, don't torment yourself if the winning set continues without you. In all likelihood it won't continue long. If it does, console yourself by thinking of all the times when selling too soon preserved gains you would otherwise have lost.

The Third Major Axiom:
ON HOPE

When the ship starts to sink, don't pray. Jump.

The Second Axiom was all about what to do when things are going right. The Third Axiom is about saving yourself when they go wrong.

And they surely will go wrong. You can depend on it. You can expect that roughly half your speculative ventures will turn sour before you have reached your preplanned ending positions. Half your guesses about the future will be wrong. Half your judgments of economic forces will be inaccurate. Half the advice you hear will be bad.

Half your hopes are doomed never to be realized.

But cheer up. This doesn't mean you are bound to lose a dollar for every dollar you gain. If that were true, the whole adventure would be pointless. It is true only of the inept. Successful gamblers and speculators handle things better. They forge ahead in large measure because they know what to do, *and unhesitatingly do it,* when the tide of events turns against them.

Knowing how to get out of a bad situation may be the rarest of all speculative gifts. It is rare because it is difficult to acquire. It takes courage and a kind of honesty with a cutting edge like a razor blade. It is an ability that separates the men and women from the boys and girls. Some say it is the most important of all the tools in a gambler's or speculator's kit.

One man who would agree with that statement is Martin Schwartz, a former securities analyst who now spends full time speculating in commodity futures. (Most full-timers prefer to call it "trading," but we'll stick with our own word.) In 1983, Schwartz increased his playing money by a spectacular 175 percent. That made him the winner of the U.S. Trading Championship, an annual contest sponsored by a Chicago commodity brokerage—and it also made him a lot wealthier. Asked how he achieved such nice results, Schwartz focused instantly on the one ability he felt to be essential. "I'll tell you how I became a winner," he told the *New York Times*. "I learned how to lose."

You hear almost identical words around gambling casinos. Asked what makes a good poker player, Sherlock Feldman answered without hesitating, "Knowing when to fold."

An amateur gambler hopes or prays the cards will fall his way, but a professional studies how he will save himself when they fall against him. That is probably the major difference between the two. It helps explain why a pro can expect to earn his living at the poker table, while an amateur (if playing against pros) can expect to get taken to the cleaner's every time he plays.

The inability to jump quickly off a sinking ship has probably cost more speculators more money than any other failing, and has undoubtedly led to the spilling of more gallons of tears than any other kind of financial misfortune. "Getting stuck in a losing venture is the worst money pain there is," says Susan Garner, who recently quit her job with the Chase Manhattan Bank in order to devote full time to speculation. She is successful now, but she wasn't always. It took her time to learn the techniques—particularly to learn how to lose.

In one of her earliest ventures, she recalls, she paid $2,000 for a fractional interest in a small suburban office building. The building was situated in a somewhat sleepy community that seemed on the point of waking up. A major federal-state highway was scheduled to be built in the region, and the planned route took it along one border of the town. Because of the projected highway and certain other economic and geographic factors, everybody expected that the town would develop into a thriving commercial center. When that happens to a community, of course, real estate values often rise rapidly—including the value of office space. Susan Garner's speculation looked promising.

But as often happens, the future was postponed. The highway project was hit by funding problems. A series of announcements spoke of longer and longer delays. At first the official word was that the project would be postponed for about a year. Then it was two or three years, then five years. Finally a state official found the courage to tell the truth: He honestly didn't know when the highway would be built, if ever.

With each succeeding announcement, the fever of real estate speculation cooled a bit. There were no daily price quotations on Susan Garner's little piece of a building, but she didn't need precise numbers to tell her she was getting poorer. She thought of selling out.

"There were people who would have bought my share," she says. "But I knew I'd have to sell at a loss, and I couldn't bring myself to do it. After the first announcement of a one-year delay in the highway, I tried to tell myself everything would be okay if I just sat tight. This was just a temporary setback —that's what I kept saying. All I had to do was wait, and my share value would go back up."

Then came the announcement of a two- or three-year delay. One of the bigger shareholders in the office building, a lawyer, now approached Susan Garner and offered her $1,500 for her share. She could not bear the thought of losing $500—one-fourth of her investment—and she turned him down. He raised his offer to $1,600. She still said no.

As the announced delays stretched toward infinity, the price fell steeply. The lawyer offered her $1,000. A little later he was down to $800. The lower the price dropped, the more tightly Susan Garner felt stuck. "Now I wasn't even hoping to get my $2,000 back," she says. "I was angry at myself for not taking $1,500 when I could have gotten it. I kept hoping the situation would improve and vindicate my judgment. The lower the price went, the more stubborn I got. I was *damned* if I was going to sell my $2,000 share for a lousy $800!"

While her money was trapped in this souring venture, other speculations beckoned. She wanted to take a flier in antique furniture. She liked the look of the stock market. A friend wanted to sell, at a bargain price, an inherited album of rare nineteenth-century postage stamps, and this attracted her too. But the trapped $2,000 was the bulk of her speculating capital. She could hardly make a move until she freed it.

"I finally decided," she says, "that it was ridiculous to let money get frozen up like that." She sold her share for $750.

And that was how Susan Garner learned the lesson of the Third Axiom. When the ship starts to sink, jump.

Note the wording: when it *starts* to sink. Don't wait until it is half submerged. Don't hope, don't pray. Don't cover your eyes and stand there trembling. Look around at what's happening. Study the situation. Ask yourself whether the developing problem is likely to get fixed. Look for trustworthy and tangible evidence that improvement is on the way, and if you see none, take action without further delay. Calmly and deliberately, before everybody else has started to panic, jump off the ship and save yourself.

This advice can be translated into numbers in the case of daily-traded entities such as stocks or commodity futures. Gerald Loeb's rule of thumb was that you should sell whenever a stock's price has retreated 10 to 15 percent from the highest price at which you have held it, regardless of whether you then have a gain or a loss. Frank Henry gave himself a bit more leeway and said 10 to 20 percent. Most seasoned speculators operate with very similar rules. In all cases, the idea is to cut losses early. *You take small losses to protect yourself from big ones.*

To illustrate, let's suppose you've bought some stock at $100 a share. The venture immediately turns sour; the price drops to $85. In this case the highest price at which you ever held the stock was the price at which you bought it: $100. You're down 15 percent from that level, so the rules say you probably ought to sell. As long as you see no good evidence that some kind of improvement is in the works, get out.

Or let's take a happier case. You buy the stock at $100, and it jumps to $120. You're going to get rich, you think. Oh frabjous day! But then some unexpected trouble hits the company, and your stock sags back to $100. What should you do? You know the answer by now. In the absence of compelling reasons to think things will get better, sell.

But knowing the answer is only half the battle. There are three obstacles that get in people's way when they are trying to carry out the precept of the Third Axiom. For some speculators, the obstacles are intimidatingly big. You must prepare yourself psychologically to face them. They can be overcome if you keep your cool.

The first obstacle is the fear of regret—substantially the same fear we looked at under the Second Axiom. In this case, what you fear is that a loser will turn into a winner after you've gone away.

It does happen, and it hurts. You've bought some gold at $400 an ounce, let's say. It collapses to $350. Seeing no good reason to stick around, you decide to take your 12 percent loss and sell out. No sooner is the transaction completed than six new wars break out, four South American countries default on their international debt, the OPEC nations double the price of oil, all the world's stock markets crash, and everybody with spare dollars is rushing for the protection of the yellow metal. The price zooms to $800. Ouch!

Yes, it hurts. It probably will happen to you sooner or later. There is no way to avoid it. But such sudden reversals of fortune do not happen often. More frequently, a situation that goes bad will stay bad, at least for a while. The problems that cause significant price drops in speculative entities—stocks, commodities, real estate—tend to be long-lived problems. They are slow to develop and slow to go away. More often than not, the correct course is to bail out when a price first develops an appreciable sag.

There are some situations in human life, it is true, in which it may seem wiser to wait out bad times. But that is seldom a wise course where your money is concerned. If you let it get stuck in a bad venture, and if the problems last, you can go for years without having the use of that money. It's locked up when, instead, it should be out chasing gains for you in other, livelier ventures.

The second obstacle to implementation of the Third Axiom is the need to abandon part of an investment. This is inordinately painful to some. To console you, however, I can tell you that it gets less painful with practice.

You're speculating in currencies, we'll say, and you've put $5,000 into a bet on Italian lire. Your hunch has proved wrong, the exchange rates have turned against you, and your extractable capital has shrunk to $4,000. You probably ought to sell out as long as no definite promise of improvement is in sight. But if you do sell out, you abandon $1,000. That is what hurts.

It hurts some so much that they cannot do it. The instinct of the typical small-time speculator is to sit tight, hoping to get that $1,000 back someday. If you don't conquer that instinct, you may remain a small-time speculator—or become a bankrupt one. The way to get that grand back is to pull your $4,000 out of the sagging venture and put it into a livelier one.

The inability to abandon part of an investment becomes twice as bad a problem if you speculate on margin—that is, use borrowed money to boost your leverage. Your speculative situation then comes to resemble the most exquisitely agonizing game in the world, poker.

It will be worthwhile to explore this resemblance briefly. Indeed, you will find it extremely rewarding to study the game of poker if you aren't already familiar with it. Get into some Friday-night neighborhood games, or organize some. Poker is designed to test some elements of human character to their very limits. You have much to learn from the game—about speculation and about yourself.

When you speculate on a cash basis—that is, when you don't use any borrowed money—life is relatively simple. You buy some stock, let's say. You pay cash on the barrelhead. You aren't required to do more than make that single investment. If the stock's price sinks and you fail to bail out, being unwilling to abandon whatever money you've lost, you aren't asked to *do* anything. All that happens is that you sit and watch morosely while your wealth shrinks. Nobody asks you to throw *more* money into the venture.

Now consider poker. In a poker hand, you must keep adding to your investment if you want to stay in the game. You're drawing to a flush, we'll say. The odds are against you; the hand is a probable loser. But you've invested a lot of money in the pot so far and you can't make yourself abandon it. Against your better judgment (and the teaching of the Third Axiom) you elect to stay.

This isn't an ordinary cash-basis speculation, however. This is poker. If you stay, you pay. If you want to see that next card, you must buy it. The game requires that you continually invest new money to protect old money.

Speculation on margin produces similar agony. You buy some stock, borrowing a certain percentage of the price from your broker. The allowable percentage is determined by government regulations, stock-exchange rules, and individual brokerage policies. The stock is held by the broker as collateral for the loan. If the stock's trading price drops, its value as collateral, obviously, will also drop. This can put you in automatic violation of the rules about margin percentages. You will then receive the dreaded "margin call"—a friendly but no-nonsense communication in which your broker offers you two hard choices: Either you come up with more cash to cover the discrepancy, or he sells you out.

You are in substantially the same position as the poker player. If you aren't willing to abandon part of your investment, then you must throw more money into the pot.

The willingness to abandon is usually the more trustworthy response. If you don't sense or can't cultivate this willingness in yourself, speculation of any kind could be difficult for you, and speculation on margin could be disastrous.

The third obstacle to the Third Axiom's implementation is the difficulty of admitting you were wrong. People differ widely in the ways they react to this problem. Some find it only a minor nuisance. Some find it the biggest obstacle of all. Women tend to overcome it more readily than men, older people more readily than younger. I don't have any idea why this is so, and neither does anybody else, including those who say they do. Let's leave it at this: It is a tall obstacle for many. If you feel it will get in your way, you should explore yourself and seek ways to handle it.

You make an investment, it turns sour, you know you ought to get out. But in order to do that, you must admit you made a mistake. You must admit it to your broker or banker or whomever you've been dealing with, maybe to your spouse and other family members—and, usually worst of all, to yourself. You've got to stand there in front of a mirror, look yourself in the eye, and say, "I was wrong."

For some, that is impossibly painful. The typical loser tries to avoid the pain and, as a result, repeatedly gets trapped in bad ventures. If he buys something whose price begins to sag, he hangs on in the hope that future events will vindicate his judgment. "This price drop is just temporary," he tells himself —and maybe even believes it. "I was right to get into this speculation. It would be foolish to sell out just because of some initial bad luck. I'll sit tight. Time will show how smart I am!"

Thus does he protect his ego. He has evaded the necessity of saying he was wrong. He can go on believing he is smart.

His bankbook will record the truth, however. Years from now, perhaps, that sagging investment will struggle back to the price at which he bought it or will even go higher, and then he will feel vindicated. "I was right all along!" he will exult. But was he? During all those years while his money was stagnating, it could have been out working. He could have doubled it or better. Instead, he stands just about where he stood at the beginning of this dismal episode.

Refusing to be wrong is the wrongest response of them all.

MINOR AXIOM IV.
Accept small losses cheerfully as a fact
of life. Expect to experience several while
awaiting a large gain.

Ideally we should welcome our small losses, since they protect us from large losses. That is asking too much, however. *Wel-*

come a loss? I never met anybody who could or did. But if we can't do that, we can at least accept those small losses with good grace.

They really provide excellent protection. If you habitually cut your losses in the ways we've discussed, you aren't likely ever to be badly hurt. The only way you can get caught in a market crash is to get taken by surprise and then to find you can't sell when you want to. This can happen in some non-liquid speculative worlds such as real estate or antiques, where you must protect yourself by careful and constant study of changing market conditions. You are less likely to get accidentally trapped in the case of daily-traded entities such as stocks or commodity futures, where you can almost always find somebody making a market in whatever you want to sell.

Get in the habit of taking small losses. If a venture doesn't work out, walk away and try something else. Don't sit on a sinking ship. Don't get trapped.

"All things come to him who waits," says an ancient Chinese proverb. If the ancient Chinese believed that, they cannot have been very good speculators. You certainly should not believe it, for at least as it applies to the world of money, it is perfect nonsense. If you wait for sagging ventures to improve, you are doomed to frequent disappointment—and doomed, too, to remain unrich.

The most productive attitude—admittedly not an easy one to achieve—is to expect small losses the way you expect any other less than pleasant fact of financial life. The way you expect taxes, for instance, or electric bills. Your annual waltz with the Internal Revenue Service isn't fun by any definition, but you probably don't let it unhinge you. You say, "Well, all right, this is all part of earning a living. This is what it costs." Try to think of small losses that way. They are part of the cost of speculation. They buy you the right to hope for big gains.

Some speculators prepare for small losses in advance through use of stop-loss orders. A stop-loss order is a standing instruction to your broker: If the stock which you have bought at $100 ever falls to $90, or any other level you designate, he is to sell you out automatically.

Some find stop-loss orders useful and others don't. The main advantage is that such an order saves you from the agony of deciding when to sell. It puts you in a frame of mind to accept the loss if and when it occurs. You think, "Okay, I'm going into this venture with $10,000. The least it can shrink to is $9,000, less brokerage commissions." That's comforting. In time, with luck, you come to think of $9,000 as the base. If the broker has to sell you out, you don't feel as though any significant loss at all has occurred.

The disadvantage is that a stop-loss order robs you of flexibility. There are some situations in which you might think it sensible to dump that stock at $90, but others in which it might make more sense to hold to $85. With a stop-loss order on the books, you tend to stop thinking.

Stop-loss services are available only with certain daily-traded entities such as stocks and commodities, and many brokerages offer the service only to accounts over a certain size. If you are a speculator in rare coins or antiques, only one person in the world is going to help you with your loss-taking, and that person is you.

My own opinion is that you are better off operating without any automatic loss-taking mechanism. Depend instead on your own capacity to reach hard decisions and follow them through. You may be amazed at how tough you can become with a little practice—and that will be an extra reward of the risk-taker's way of life.

You and your bank account can both grow larger simultaneously.

Speculative Strategy

The Third Axiom tells you not to wait around when trouble shows itself. It tells you to get away promptly.

Don't hope, don't pray. Hope and prayer are nice, no doubt, but they are not useful as tools of a speculative operation.

Nobody pretends it is easy to carry out the teaching of this hard, unsentimental Axiom. We've looked at three obstacles to its implementation: fear of regret, unwillingness to abandon part of an investment, and difficulty of admitting a mistake. One or more of these problems may afflict you, perhaps severely. Somehow or other, you have to overcome them.

The Axioms are about speculation, not psychological self-help, and therefore they have no advice to offer on *how* you overcome these obstacles. That is an internal and individual process; the *how* is probably different for each of us. The Third Axiom says only that learning to take losses is an essential speculative technique. The fact that most men and women fail to learn the technique is one of the key reasons why most are not good speculators or gamblers.

The Fourth Major Axiom:
ON FORECASTS

Human behavior cannot be predicted. Distrust anyone who claims to know the future, however dimly.

Back in 1969, when the Consumer Price Index rose by about 5 percent, the consensus of leading economists was that the inflation rate would rise a bit in the early 1970s but then would taper off later in the decade. It didn't. It doubled.

In 1979, when the index leaped by a scorching 11½ percent, the consensus of the seers was that the rate would stay at double-digit levels through the mid-1980s. It didn't. It was back down to 1969's peaceful levels by 1982.

It makes you wonder. Why do we go on listening to economic prophets when they plainly know no more about the future than you or I?

We listen, no doubt, because knowledge of the future is and has always been one of the most desperately sought human goals. If you could read tomorrow's stock prices today, you would be rich. And so we listen with respect and hope anytime somebody stands up and announces a vision of things to come.

More often than not, listening turns out to be a mistake. Back in the summer of 1929, on August 23, the *Wall Street Journal* told its readers they could make a lot of money in the stock market. The *Journal's* special crystal ball, a future-gazing technique called the Dow Theory, revealed that "a major upward trend" had been established in stock prices. "The outlook for the fall months seems brighter than at any time," the *Journal* warbled happily. A couple of months later, everybody went down the drain.

In more modern times, stock market guru Joseph Granville determined early in 1981 that stock prices were about to collapse. "Sell everything!" he instructed the thousands of disciples who subscribed to his advisory service. The expected collapse didn't happen. The market seesawed through 1981. Granville remained bearish. The following year, 1982, saw the start of a spectacular bull market, one of the biggest and most sudden in living memory. People who got left behind by that market came to regret it earnestly.

Granville wasn't alone in failing to foresee the bull market or in predicting its opposite. The year 1983 was a particularly dismal one for financial oracles. Consider the record of money managers—the professionals who handle "investment" (or, as we would rather call it, speculation) for insurance companies, pension funds, and the like. In 1983, according to an estimate by the *New York Times*, three-fifths of these high-paid seers were so wrong in their guesses about the future that they made less money than would a novice speculator making choices by throwing dice.

The most commonly used measure of investment performance is Standard & Poor's index of 500 common stocks. In 1983 this index rose some 22 percent. To put it another way, if you had a 22 percent gain on your speculative portfolio that year, you were doing average work. The performance would rate you a grade of C. According to the *Times* survey, 60 percent of money managers did *worse* than that.

There was one once-celebrated manager, for example, who predicted that interest rates would fall in 1983, so he invested heavily in bonds. Interest rates rose, and as a result the value of all those fixed-interest bonds plunged. The same man thought drug-company stocks would rise, but they fell. He thought projected changes in the telephone industry would be of particular benefit to MCI, so he loaded his clients' portfolios with that company's stock. It turned out to be a dog.

The fact is, nobody has the faintest idea of what is going to happen next year, next week, or even tomorrow. If you hope to get anywhere as a speculator, you must get out of the habit of listening to forecasts. It is of the utmost importance that you never take economists, market advisers, or other financial oracles seriously.

Of course, they are right sometimes, and that is what makes them dangerous. Each of them, after being in the prophecy business for a few years, can point proudly to a few guesses that turned out right. "Amazing!" everybody says. What never appears in the prophet's publicity is a reminder of all the times when he or she was wrong.

"It's easy to be a prophet," the noted economist Dr. Theodore Levitt once told *Business Week*. "You make twenty-five predictions and the ones that come true are the ones you talk about." Not many seers are that frank, but all would privately agree with Dr. Levitt's formula for success. Economists, market advisers, political oracles, and clairvoyants all know the basic rule by heart: If you can't forecast right, forecast often.

You can watch economists assiduously obeying this rule every year. Every June or July, the top prophets start issuing their solemn guesses about the first quarter of the year to come. The guesses usually deal with the big index numbers: the GNP, the inflation rate, the prime rate, and so on. Since they obviously study each other's predictions with care, there tends often to be a remarkable uniformity in what they foresee. Many speculators base decisions on these guesses—and so do mighty corporations and the U.S. government.

Around September each year, the economic scene looks

somewhat different, so the economists all come out with "revised" forecasts about the coming first quarter.

Around November, things have changed still more, so we are treated to re-revised forecasts. In December . . . well, you get the picture. Each oracle prays that at least one of his predictions will be right. The later ones are the more likely to be on target, since they are closer to the period being prognosticated, but occasionally one of the earlier forecasts hits the mark. The prophet will then make a virtue of the fact: "I foresaw this back in July!"

He will carefully avoid mentioning that his correct forecast was supposedly canceled and superseded by revised and double-revised predictions that he issued later on.

As for you and me, lone speculators trying to make a buck, we are well advised to ignore the whole ballet. If the June forecasts are going to be superseded by September ones, and they by still more sets in November and December, why listen at all? Accepting such a prophecy is like buying a ticket that is scheduled to expire before the play is performed.

Not all oracles have been able to organize the annual forecast-revising dance of the economists, but all are followers of the basic rule. They all forecast often and hope nobody scrutinizes the results too carefully.

It has always been thus. Michel de Nostredame, an obscure sixteenth-century French doctor, turned out hundreds of prophecies in the form of tangled four-line verses. He is known today by the Latin form of his name, Nostradamus, and is revered by a cult of believers. He is supposed to have predicted things such as air warfare and radio communication.

Well, maybe. The verses are in such indirect, mystical language that you can interpret any of them to prove anything you want to prove. Leaning over backward to be charitable to the ancient seer, I once studied a hundred of his prognostications and ended with the following statistical summary: Three forecasts were correct, eighteen were incorrect, and the remaining seventy-nine were such dense gibberish that I simply didn't know what the old Frenchman was driving at.

Not a very impressive record. Yet Nostradamus managed to make a name for himself in the world of prophecy—a name that any modern oracle would love to equal.

Nostradamus wasn't often right, but he sure was often.

Or take a modern future-gazer, the self-advertised psychic Jeane Dixon. She is famed for some right guesses, principally one: a prediction of President Kennedy's assassination. Amazing, right? Sure, but what isn't so well publicized is a list of all her wrong guesses. According to Ruth Montgomery, Mrs. Dixon's biographer-disciple, the renowned clairvoyant predicted that Russia and China would unite under one ruler, that CIO chief Walter Reuther would run for President, that a cure for cancer would grow out of research begun early in this century, that . . .

Well, you see the point. The Committee for Scientific Investigation of Claims of the Paranormal, a scholarly group based at the State University of New York at Buffalo, studied Jeane Dixon's record and found it to be no better than that of an ordinary man or woman making guesses.

It is easy to get dazzled by a successful prophet, for there is a hypnotic allure in the supposed ability to look into the future. This is especially true in the world of money. A seer who enjoys a few years of frequently right guesses will attract an enormous following—so big a following, in some cases, that the seer's prophecies are sometimes self-fulfilling.

Such was the case with Joseph Granville, the stock market oracle. So many people were basing decisions on Granville's forecasts in the early 1980s that when he said something was going to happen, it happened because they believed it would. That is, when he said the market would go down, the prediction scared buyers out of the market—and lo, it went down.

This happened early in 1981, when Granville told his disciples to sell everything. The day after this famous warning was issued, the stock market fell out of bed—23 points on the Dow. All of Wall Street said *ooh* and *ah*. What a powerful prophet was this Granville! The plunge was brief but impressive while it lasted.

If you had then been a student of the Zurich Axioms, it might have seemed to you that here was an exception to the teaching of the Fourth Axiom. Though most prophecies aren't worth two cents, might it not be a good idea to put one's money on a seer like Granville? If his forecasts are self-fulfilling, aren't you all but sure to win by doing what he recommends?

No. Not even self-fulfilling prophecies self-fulfill reliably. Later in 1981, Granville launched another test of his prophetic power. His crystal ball told him the market would plunge again on Monday, September 28. He announced this to the world. Some speculators sold stock short or bought puts on the strength of it. They, like Granville, were convinced the plunge was coming.

Instead, the New York Stock Exchange that day scored one of the biggeat price gains in its history, and a day later, markets in Europe and Japan followed suit.

Some of Granville's followers were baffled, but they need not have been. They had merely had it demonstrated to them that Granville is like anybody else: He wins some and he loses some.

Every prophet is right sometimes and wrong sometimes—more often the latter, but you can't tell in advance which it is going to be. To be in a position to tell, you would have to make predictions about the prophet's predictions. If you were that good at predicting, you wouldn't need the prophet. Since you aren't that good at it, you can't count on anything the seer says.

So you might as well forget the whole fruitless exercise of trying to catch a glimpse of the future.

Let's look at another example. Back in 1970 a financial editor, columnist, and oracle named Donald I. Rogers published a book entitled *How to Beat Inflation by Using It*. This book was notable for containing the magnificently wrong advice that one should not buy gold. However, we can forgive Rogers that forecasting failure. Gold was a common blind spot in crystal balls of the time. What is more interesting is this prophet's listing of common stocks that he thought would do well in the years ahead.

Rogers reasoned that land would be a good hedge against inflation. Therefore, he figured, it would be a good idea to buy stocks of companies that owned a lot of land. He listed stocks to buy on that basis.

Some of his recommendations have turned out pretty well in the years since. Warner Communications, for instance. If you had bought this stock in 1970, you could have sold out at a handsome profit at various times until trouble struck the company in mid-1983. Other recommendations on Rogers's list, such as ITT, have turned out miserably.

The question is: If you had read Rogers's survival manual in 1970 and accepted some of his prognostications, how would you have fared?

Well, it would have depended on your luck. If you had picked winners from his list, you would have won, and if you had picked losers, you would have lost. Luck was in control of the outcome all the time. That being so, one can ask what was the sense of listening to the prophet in the first place.

It may seem unfair to pillory Rogers and other oracles on the basis of hindsight. It is easy, after all, to sit here today and say what was and wasn't a good speculation in the 1970s. A prophet might be excused, perhaps, for challenging me: "See here, Gunther, what gives you the right to catalog all our wrong guesses? Could you do better? Are you such a hot prophet?"

Ah, a good question. No, I'm not a prophet, and that is just the point. I've never made any serious attempt to read the future (though of course I'm always wondering about it), have never said I *could* read the future, and indeed have just spent many pages saying it can't be done. But the people we've been criticizing here are men and women who claim they *can* see ahead. They have set themselves up as oracles, they accept money for their prognostications, and they are aware, or should be, that there are people who reach important decisions on the basis of what they say. It seems perfectly proper, therefore, to hold these prophets accountable for what they predict. If they are selling a prediction service, we have a right to subject that service to critical scrutiny and find out how good it is.

The conclusion is that it isn't very good. You cannot profit by listening to a prophet.

There are things that can be predicted. We know precisely when the sun is going to come up each morning, for instance. Tide tables are prepared months ahead. The free calendar I get each January from the bank says what the moon's phases will be throughout the twelve months ahead. Weather forecasts are less precise but still are reasonably trustworthy and getting more so.

The reason why such things can be predicted, and why the predictions can be trusted, is that they are physical events. But the Zurich Axioms are about the world of money, and that is a world of human events. Human events absolutely cannot be predicted, by any method, by anybody.

One of the traps money-world prophets fall into is that they forget they are dealing with human behavior. They talk as though things like the inflation rate or the ups and downs of the Dow are physical events of some kind. Looking at such a phenomenon as a physical event, an oracle can understandably succumb to the illusion that it will be amenable to forecasting. The fact is, of course, that all money phenomena are manifestations of human behavior.

The stock market, for example, is a colossal engine of human emotion. Prices of stocks rise and fall because of what men and women are doing, thinking, and feeling. The price of a given company's shares doesn't rise because of abstract figures in an accounting ledger, nor even because the company's future prospects are objectively good, but because people *think* the prospects are good. The market doesn't slump because a computer somewhere determines selling pressure is on the rise, but because people are worried, or discouraged, or afraid. Or simply because a four-day weekend is coming and all the buyers are off for the seashore.

It is the same with all those grand index numbers economists love to play with: the GNP, housing starts, the inflation rate. All are the results of human interaction, men and women striving restlessly in the eternal battle for survival and self-betterment. And it is the same with the end results of those index phenomena fermenting together: recessions and recoveries and booms, good times and bad. All are caused by people.

And as such, all are entirely unpredictable.

There are simply too many unknowable variables involved to allow for trustworthy forecasts of something like the inflation rate. The rate is caused by millions of people making billions of decisions: workers about wages they want to be paid, bosses about wages they are willing to pay, consumers about prices they will swallow, everybody about diffuse feelings of hardship or prosperity, fear or security, discontent or buoyancy. To claim you can make reliable forecasts about this staggering complexity seems arrogant to the point of being ridiculous.

As the Axiom says, human behavior cannot be predicted.

Since all money-world forecasts are about human behavior, you should not take any of them seriously.

Taking them seriously can lead you into many a dark and gloomy valley. The stock market probably offers some of the most stark examples. To pick one at random, consider the *Value Line Investment Survey*'s 1983 forecast about the Apple Computer Company.

Value Line sells a regular oracular service in which it periodically rates stocks for what it calls "performance" over the coming twelve months. In other words, it gazes into the future of each stock and says what it thinks will happen to the stock's price in the year ahead.

It must be said that Value Line's record has been pretty good in most recent years. However, we are up against the same problem we discussed in connection with Donald I. Rogers and his list of stocks to buy in 1970. If you were a Value Line subscriber and accepted the forecasts as gospel, your personal financial fate would depend on whether you were lucky enough to act on the good prophecies while passing the bad ones by.

And there sure have been some bad ones. One of the most spectacularly bad was the prophecy about Apple Computer.

On July 1, 1983, Value Line published a list of "Selected Stocks for Performance." One company on this elite list was Apple. Its shares were then trading in the neighborhood of $55. A few months later they were down to 17¼.

The debacle was caused, of course, by events that Value Line could not foresee in July. An oracle can always cry "unforeseeable events" in explanation of a forecast that turns out wrong. But that is just the trouble. *Every* forecast has the possibility of unforeseeable events ahead of it. No forecast about human behavior can ever be compounded of 100 percent foreseeable events. Every prediction is chancy. None can ever be trusted.

Many of those who bought Apple in July 1983 must have sold

out before it hit bottom. Some, acting according to the Third Axiom, may have jumped ship with only minor losses. But there are situations in which such early abandonment isn't possible. A bad forecast can, if you aren't wary, get you trapped in a losing proposition for years.

Consider all the poor folks, for example, who bought long-term certificates of deposit from banks in the early to middle 1970s. As we noted earlier, economists had predicted that interest rates would rise at the beginning of that decade and then level out or taper off. The first part of the prediction turned out right. Rates rose. Banks began offering four-year and six-year CDs with unheard-of interest rates like 7 and 8 percent.

To earn those huge rates — huge as seen from the viewpoint of the early 1970s — you were, of course, required to kiss your money goodbye for the stated number of years. You couldn't withdraw it except by special arrangement and under pain of a stiff penalty. How did bankers get people to let their money be locked up like that? The bankers did it by reiterating the economists' prediction.

"Look, you're gonna get 7 percent!" a banker would tell a prospective depositor couple, standing there with their life savings clutched in trembling hands. "Where did you ever hear of a rate like that before? Can you *imagine* getting more? It'll never happen! What you want to do is grab it while you can get it. All the top economists say rates will go down next year or the year after, and our own people agree. Lock in that 7 percent and you'll be sitting pretty!"

It sounded great. Until the prediction turned out wrong.

Rates went up to levels that nobody had ever dreamed of before. By the end of the decade, banks were offering six-month CDs with rates in the eye-popping range of 10 and 11 percent.

Those high-paying six-monthers were very popular. A lot of people wanted them. Including many whose money was serving a six-year sentence at 7 percent.

Speculative Strategy

The Fourth Axiom tells you not to build your speculative program on a basis of forecasts, because it won't work. Disregard all prognostications. In the world of money, which is a world shaped by human behavior, nobody has the foggiest notion of what will happen in the future. Mark that word. *Nobody*.

Of course, we all wonder what will happen, and we all worry about it. But to seek escape from that worry by leaning on predictions is a formula for poverty. The successful speculator bases no moves on what supposedly *will* happen but reacts instead to what *does* happen.

Design your speculative program on the basis of quick reactions to events that you can actually see developing in the present. Naturally, in selecting an investment and committing money to it, you harbor the hope that its future will be bright. The hope is presumably based on careful study and hard thinking. Your act of committing dollars to the venture is itself a prediction of sorts. You are saying, "I have reason to hope this will succeed." But don't let that harden into an oracular pronouncement: "It is bound to succeed because interest rates will come down." Never, never lose sight of the possibility that you have made a bad bet.

If the speculation does succeed and you find yourself climbing toward a planned ending position, fine, stay with it. If it turns sour despite what all the prophets have promised, remember the Third Axiom. Get out.

The Fifth Major Axiom:
ON PATTERNS

Chaos is not dangerous until it begins to look orderly.

Irving Fisher, a distinguished professor of economics at Yale, made a bundle on the stock market. Impressed by his combination of impeccable academic credentials and practical investment savvy, people flocked to him for advice. "Stock prices have reached what looks like a permanently high plateau," he announced in September 1929, just before he was wiped out by the worst crash in Wall Street history.

It just goes to show you. The minute you think you see an orderly design in the affairs of men and women, including their financial affairs, you are in peril.

Fisher believed he had beaten the market by being smart, when what had really happened was that he had been lucky. He thought he saw patterns amid the chaos. Believing that, he believed it should be possible to develop formulas and strategies for the profitable exploitation of those patterns—and he believed, further, that he had in fact developed just such formulas and strategies.

Poor old Fisher. Fate let him ride high for a while so he would have farther to fall. For a few years his illusion of order seemed to be justified by the facts. "See!" he would say. "It is as

I determined. The stock market is behaving just the way I calculated it would."

And then—whomp! The bottom dropped out. Clinging to his illusion of order, Fisher was unprepared for his streak of luck to end. He and a lot of other misguided investors went tumbling down the drain.

The trap that caught Professor Fisher, the illusion of order, has caught millions of others and will go on catching investors, speculators, and gamblers for all eternity. It awaits the unwary not only around Wall Street but in art galleries, realty offices, gambling casinos, antique auctions: wherever money is wagered and lost. It is an entirely understandable illusion. After all, what is more orderly than money? No matter how disarrayed the world gets, four quarters always make a buck. Money seems cool, rational, amenable to reasoned analysis and manipulation. If you want to get rich, it would seem that you need only find a sound rational approach. A Formula.

Everybody is looking for this Formula. Unfortunately, there isn't one.

The truth is that the world of money is a world of patternless disorder, utter chaos. Patterns seem to appear in it from time to time, as do patterns in a cloudy sky or in the froth at the edge of the ocean. But they are ephemeral. They are not a sound basis on which to base one's plans. They are alluring, and they are always fooling smart people like Professor Fisher. But the really smart speculator will recognize them for what they are and, hence, will disregard them.

This is the lesson of the Fifth Axiom. It may be the most important Axiom of them all. It is the Emperor Axiom. Once you grasp it, you will be a cleverer speculator/investor than Professor Fisher was with all his vast scholarly attainments. This one Axiom, once you make it yours, will by itself lift you above the common herd of hopeful blunderers and losers.

Some of the grandest illusions of order crop up in the world of art. This is a world in which a great deal of money can be made with stunning speed. The trick is to latch on to low-priced artists before they get hot. Like Louise Moillon, a seventeenth-century French painter. A woman recently bought a Moillon at a rural auction for $1,500. Within a year Moillon got hot, and the same painting sold in New York for $120,000.

That would be a nice adventure to have. It could give one's balance sheet an encouraging boost. But how can you get in on the action? How can you tell when an obscure artist is going to attract that kind of attention?

Well, there are experts who say they have art pretty well figured out. They see patterns nobody else sees. They have formulas. They can recognize Great Art while it is still unrecognized and cheap. They can go to a rural auction where everybody else is stumbling around in the dark and say, "Wow! Look at that! It'll fetch six figures next year in New York!" So your best bet is to consult a lot of these experts, right?

Sure. The Sovereign American Art Fund was founded on that basis. It was essentially a unit trust. It proposed to make its shareholders rich by buying and selling works of art. This buying and selling was to be done by experts, savvy professionals whose superior critical judgment could help them spot emerging trends and future Moillons before the rest of the art-buying world caught the scent.

A lovely illusion of order. It attracted investors big and small. The Fund sold out its initial public offering at $6 a share.

What nobody seems to have thought of is that in any game as dicey as art, a group of professionals can experience bad luck just as easily as a herd of blundering amateurs. The Sovereign Fund's purchased masterpieces looked promising at first, and a few months after the initial offering the shares were trading over $30. Some of the initial speculators made some money, at least. But then gloom descended. The purchased masterpieces turned out to be less hot than had been supposed. Obscure artists got obscurer. One expensive painting was challenged as a forgery. The shares' value plummeted. About two years after the Fund had opened for business, the trading price was 75 cents.

Wall Street unit trusts ('mutual funds' in the USA) tell the same story. They illustrate with stark clarity how futile it is to seek patterns amid the chaos—and in the end, particularly for the average small-time plunger, how dangerous.

Consider the seemingly limitless promise of unit trusts. These great agglomerations of the public's money are managed by professionals of the first magnitude. The educational attainments of these men and women are dazzling, and so are their salaries. Platoons of assistants see to their needs. Large libraries of financial fact and theory are at their disposal. Computers and other expensive gadgets take part in their cogitations. They are without a doubt the world's best-educated, best-paid, best-equipped investment theorists.

And so, if it were possible to discern usable patterns amid the disorder and develop a market-playing formula that worked, one might suppose these people would be able to do it. Indeed, they should have done it long ago.

So far, however, the formula has eluded them.

The sad fact is that unit trusts are like all other speculators: They win some and they lose some. That's the best you can say about them. All the high-voltage brainpower and all that money and all those computers have never been able to make them any cleverer or more successful than a lone plunger with an aching head and a $12.98 pocket calculator. Indeed sometimes unit trusts as a group manage to do worse than average. *Forbes* magazine once charted the performance of trusts' unit prices in some bear markets and found that nine out of ten fell as fast as or faster than stocks as a whole.

Trust managers continue searching doggedly for that magic formula, however. They search because they are paid to, and also—in many cases or most—because they genuinely believe there is a formula out there somewhere, if only they and the computers are smart enough to spot it.

You and I know, of course, that the reason why they can't find the formula is that there isn't one.

Oh sure, you can make money by investing in a unit trust—if you are lucky enough to pick the right one at the right time. What it comes down to is that buying trust units is just as risky as buying individual stocks, or art works, or whatever your chosen game may be.

Some trust managers will be luckier than others in the coming year. Some will be hot. Their unit prices will rise faster (or fall more slowly) than average. But the question is: *which ones?*

So, you see, we are back where we started. If you want to speculate in trust units, you are only dealing with the same kind of chaos you would encounter when speculating directly in stocks, art, commodities, currencies, precious metals, real estate, antiques, or poker hands. The rules of play should be the same for you whether you are in unit trusts or anything else. *Particularly* with trusts, don't be lulled into perceiving order where none exists. Keep your wits and the Axioms about you.

And keep them about you whenever you read or hear investment advice. Most advisers have some kind of orderly illusion to sell, for that is what sells.

Such an illusion is comforting and seems full of promise. Small-time investors who have been burned or feel they have missed opportunities through ignorance or fear—and who hasn't?—will flock to an adviser who offers what seems to be a plausible, orderly approach to moneymaking. But you should regard all financial advisers with skepticism, and the more cool and bankerish they seem, the more you should distrust them.

The cooler and more bankerish a man is, the less readily will he admit that he deals with chaos, has never been able to figure it out, has no hope of figuring it out, and must take his chances like everybody else.

Alfred Malabre, Jr., is one speculator who learned his lesson well. Malabre, a *Wall Street Journal* editor, sought help with his investments when he was sent on a long assignment overseas. He wanted somebody shrewd and prudent to take care of his stock portfolio for him while he was away. It wasn't a big portfolio, but naturally he wanted it protected. In case the market crashed or something while he was gone, he wanted somebody on the spot to sell him out or do whatever else seemed necessary.

So he looked around. As he tells the story in his book *Investing for Profit in the Eighties,* his eye fell on the First National City Bank of New York, now known as Citibank. Like most banks, Citibank offered a portfolio management service. If you had a lump of capital and didn't want to play with it yourself—or were temporarily unable to do so, as in Malabre's case—you turned it over to the bankers, and they would play for you. There was a fee, of course.

Well, okay, thinks Malabre to himself. This sounds like a good solution to my problem. Here's this Citibank, one of the ten or fifteen biggest banks on the face of the earth. What these guys don't know about money probably isn't worth knowing. How can I go wrong turning my little pile over to them? Where else am I going to find financial custodians more trustworthy, more prudent, more shrewd? They certainly won't lose me any money while I'm gone, and who knows—maybe they'll make me a bundle!

That was what Malabre thought.

He was suffering from a perfectly understandable illusion of order. What could be more orderly than a gigantic New York bank? An untutored lone plunger might diddle and fiddle and make a hash of a portfolio, but not a bank. A bank had to have formulas locked up in its vaults. A bank would always know what to do.

As it turned out, the bankers came close to wiping Malabre out. They bought him a bunch of Avon Products common stock at $119 a share. Two years later it was trading under $20. They loaded him up with Sears, Roebuck at $110 and watched it sag to $41.50. They got him into IBM at just under $400, and it deflated to $151. Only by taking emergency action on his own did Malabre avert financial disaster.

That which hurts, teaches. Malabre will not soon forget the lesson he learned at Citibank. But you can learn the same lesson without getting hurt. The lesson is that you should be wary of any adviser who, looking around at the investment scene, claims to see anything but chaos. The more orderly it looks to the adviser, the less does this man or woman merit your trust.

When you put your trust in an illusion of order, you lull yourself into a dangerous sleep. There is no Zurich Axiom saying specifically that you should stay awake, but the need to do so is implicit in all the Axioms. Don't let yourself nod off. You could wake up and find your money going down the drain.

If you want to spend an instructive and entertaining afternoon watching illusions of order being constructed, go to your local library and sample the how-to-get-rich books. Even a small library is likely to have a shelf or two of them. You will find a wide variety of investment ventures represented—including, perhaps, some that appeal to you personally. How to get rich in real estate. How to hit the jackpot in rare coins.

Killings in the philately business. Stocks, bonds, gold and silver
. . . the list goes on and on.

Notice a characteristic of these books. Most of them were
written by men and women who claim they themselves were
enriched by the given schemes. *How I Got Fat on Pork Bellies*
goes the typical title.

Are these advisers telling the truth? Well, yes: the truth as
they interpret it.

There is no reason to be unnecessarily cynical about this. We
can assume we are being given an honest account in nearly
every case: The adviser worked the scheme and banked a bundle. However, we are not obliged to let ourselves be suckered
into the author's illusion of order.

He believes he got rich because he found a winning formula.
We know better. He got rich because he was lucky.

Any half-baked moneymaking scheme will work when you
are lucky. No scheme will work when you are not. Some advisers acknowledge the commanding role of luck, as do the Zurich
Axioms. The Axioms not only acknowledge it but are built on
the basic assumption that luck is the most powerful single factor in speculative success or failure.

The majority of advisers, however, ignore luck, or pretend it
isn't there, or talk their way past it as rapidly as possible. Like
the Citibank bankers, like the Sovereign American Art Fund
managers, they are in the business of selling a soothing balm:
an orderly approach, a feeling of being in control. Take my
hand, kid, don't be afraid, I know my way around. This is
how I made it. Just follow these simple step-by-step instructions. . . .

Well, you can follow them if you like, perhaps to your doom.
For a formula that worked last year isn't necessarily going to
work this year, with a different set of financial circumstances
stewing in the pot. And a formula that worked for your neigh-

bor won't necessarily work for you, with a different set of random events to contend with.

The fact is, no formula that ignores luck's dominant role can ever be trusted. This is the great, liberating truth of the Fifth Axiom.

Luck's role is illustrated not only by the fact that a given adviser can be spectacularly wrong, but by the equally telling fact that often you will find two sages giving exactly the opposite advice. For example, here on the shelf we have *How Wall Street Doubles My Money Every Three Years*, by Lewis Owen, and *The Low-High Theory of Investment*, by Samuel C. Greenfield.

Owen says you should buy stocks whose prices are nearing or have hit twelve-month highs. His illusion of order is that some kind of "momentum," as he calls it, will tend to make price movements continue. Thus, a rising stock will continue to rise.

Greenfield says you should buy stocks whose prices are nearing or have reached twelve-month lows. *His* illusion of order is that prices seesaw in a roughly predictable fashion. Thus, a stock nearing a low will soon turn upward.

Both these sages cannot be right. In fact, neither is.

The truth is that the price of a stock, or anything else you buy in hope of making a profit, will rise if you are lucky.

MINOR AXIOM V.
Beware the Historian's Trap.

The Historian's Trap is a particular kind of orderly illusion. It is based on the age-old but entirely unwarranted belief that history repeats itself. People who hold this belief—which is to say perhaps ninety-nine out of every hundred people on earth —believe as a corollary proposition that the orderly repetition of history allows for accurate forecasting in certain situations.

Thus, suppose that at some time in the past, Event A was followed by Event B. A couple of years have gone by, and now here we are witnessing Event A again. "Aha!" says nearly everybody. "Event B is about to happen!"

Don't fall into this trap. It is true that history repeats itself sometimes, but most often it doesn't, and in any case it never does so in a reliable enough way that you can prudently bet money on it.

The consequences of the Historian's Trap are usually trivial. "Whenever they're ahead at the end of the third inning, they win the game." "Every time we meet for a drink, she gets into an office crisis and turns up late." "Nobody has ever lost the New Hampshire primary and won the Presidency." People are always letting themselves be tricked by such unreliable expectations—which may be silly but isn't often dangerous. But when your money is involved, the Historian's Trap *is* dangerous, for it can wipe you out.

The trap is ubiquitous in the financial-counseling business. One might think most counselors would have learned to avoid it after observing time and again that events rarely happen the way they are expected to happen. But no—the illusion of order, or perhaps the need to believe in order, is too strong.

There are whole schools of thought around Wall Street that are based on fundamental fallacies arising out of the Historian's Trap. Stock and bond analysts will go back to the last time there was a bull market in a certain security or group of securities and collect great baskets of facts on everything that was happening around that time. They will observe that the GNP was rising, interest rates were falling, the steel industry was having a profitable year, the insurance business was in a slump, the White Sox were in the cellar, and the President's Aunt Matilda had a cold. Then they will wait until the same configuration of circumstances comes together again. "Hey wow!" they will shout when the portentous constellation appears.

"Look! Everything is in place! A new bull market is on the way!"

Maybe it is. And maybe it isn't.

Frank Henry knew a young woman who fell into the Historian's Trap headfirst and nearly perished there. She worked for the Swiss Bank Corporation in a lowly, ill-paid clerical job, and when she inherited a little mound of capital on her father's death, she resolved to invest the money and lift herself above the ranks of the neither-poor-nor-rich. Frank Henry admired her spunk, took a grandfatherly interest in her, and gave her counsel when she asked for it.

She was attracted to currency trading, having first learned about it in her bank job. This is a game of high risk but, when you win, commensurately high reward. The basis of the game is the fluid way in which the world's many currencies fluctuate in value against one another.

To play, you buy—let's say—a bundle of Japanese yen, paying in dollars. You hope the value of the yen against the dollar will rise. If it does, you happily unload your yen for more dollars than you paid. Because currency values are volatile and because the trading is commonly conducted on a basis of heavy "margin"—meaning that you put up only a relatively small amount of your own cash, borrowing the rest from a broker —your leverage is strong. You can double your money, or conversely get your financial teeth kicked in, virtually overnight.

Most small-time currency speculators play with just a few currencies, often only two. This was the young woman's approach. She felt she had a particularly good understanding of the interplay between the U.S. dollar and the Italian lira. Frank Henry applauded her decision to play just one game at a time—not a bad decision for any beginning speculator—but he got worried when he began to see her falling into the Historian's Trap.

She told him one day that she had made a thorough historical study of the dollar's and lira's ups and downs in relation to each other. Such a study can be useful in any investment situation, as long as you conduct the study without making the underlying assumption that history is going to repeat itself. Unfortunately, the young woman made just that assumption.

According to her studies, she told Frank Henry, the lira always rose against the dollar when the Swiss franc was rising, when American-Soviet relations were cool, and when several other indicators clicked into place in international economics and diplomacy. She proposed to wait until the indicators gave the historical signal, and then she would plunge into the game.

The Zurich Axioms had not been completely formulated when this was happening, so Frank Henry did not have a convenient label like "Historian's Trap" with which to identify what he felt was wrong with her thinking. He did his best to dissuade her, but she was too excited to listen. This is nearly always the case with discoverers of new moneymaking formulas. "She thought she'd found some kind of magic key," Frank Henry said sorrowfully. "I asked her why thousands of other brainy people had never found it in years of looking, but she didn't know and didn't care. She was so exicted that when a young fellow took her out to dinner at an Italian place one night, she spent half the time talking to the headwaiter about exchange rates."

Finally the international indicators said "Go!" and she went. She became the owner of a pile of lire. Which promptly began to lose value against the dollar.

"Sell!" Frank Henry urged when the young woman had lost some 15 percent of her money.

But her illusion of order was too strong. All she had to do was wait, she thought, and her formula would be proved right. The formula had always been right in the past. It couldn't be wrong now! The market was!

But she was seeing the world upside down. Formulas can be

wrong, but markets never are. The market does what it does. It makes no predictions and offers no promises. It just *is*. Arguing with it is like standing in a blizzard and howling that it wasn't supposed to arrive until tomorrow.

The young woman argued and argued. The international exchange market refused to cooperate. Frank Henry never found out how much money she lost, because he felt it would be unkind to ask. But by the time she sold out of her lira position, she had surely been to the cleaner's.

MINOR AXIOM VI.
Beware the Chartist's Illusion.

Representing numbers by lines on graph paper can be useful or dangerous. It is useful when it helps you visualize something with greater clarity than you could achieve with numbers alone. It is dangerous when it makes the thing represented look more solid and portentous than it really is.

The Chartist's Illusion is often a graphic extension of the Historian's Trap. This is best illustrated by the chartists of Wall Street. These are people with their own jargon, which hardly anybody else can understand; their own magazines and newsletters, which ditto; and their own starkly visualized illusion of order. They believe that the future price of a stock—or a currency, a precious metal, or anything else for which frequent market-price data are published—can be ascertained by charting price movements of the past.

The chartist begins by fastening his attention on a certain investment medium, let's say a stock, Hoo Boy Computer. He goes back through months or years of records showing the ups and downs in Hoo Boy's trading price, and he translates these numbers into points and lines on graph paper. He studies the resulting patterns. He looks particularly for jiggles and wiggles that occurred just before Hoo Boy stock began a significant price rise or a sharp drop. He believes these patterns will repeat themselves. The next time he sees a similar set of jiggles and wiggles, he will conclude that a new price rise or drop is on the way and will take the appropriate speculative action.

When things don't work out as he expects—which, as often as not, they don't—he will humbly blame himself. The problem, he insists, is that he hasn't been astute enough. He *knows* the market can be predicted by charting, if only he can figure out what patterns to look for.

He can't make himself believe the simplest of all possible explanations: that the stock market has no patterns. It almost never repeats itself and never does so in a reliably predictable way. Making charts of stock prices is like making charts of ocean froth. You'll see each pattern once, and then it will be gone. Only by blind chance will you ever see it again. If you do see it again it will have no significance, for it predicts nothing.

Another element of the Chartist's Illusion springs from the peculiar way in which a solid black line, boldly drawn on grid paper, can make a bunch of uninteresting and essentially disorderly numbers look like a Major Trend. The hucksters and con artists of the world have been aware of this power of the chart for centuries. Unit trust salespeople use it all the time. The value of a trust's units may have been creeping up so slowly that they haven't even kept pace with inflation, but by squeezing years close together on a chart page, and perhaps by bridging over some bad years they would prefer not to discuss, the trust's promoters can produce a honey of a chart for their sales brochure. You look at that soaring black line and say, "Wow!"

The danger is not just that you can be conned by others, but that you can hoodwink yourself. You look at a chart depicting the value of the lira against the dollar in recent years, for instance. The line slopes upward. You think, "Wow! Maybe I ought to climb aboard!"

But wait. Don't be mesmerized by the line alone. Look at the numbers it is supposed to represent. Maybe it depicts only the lira's yearly highs. Another chart showing the yearly lows might have a downward slope. In other words, the lira-dollar relationship has been marked by increasingly wide swings. The calm, steady change implied by that upward-sloping line is an illusion. The truth is that the relationship is one of increasing disorder.

In such ways do people allow themselves to be deluded by charts. A chart line always has a comfortingly orderly look, even when what it depicts is chaos.

Life never happens in a straight line. Any adult knows this. But we can too easily be hypnotized into forgetting it when contemplating a chart.

You look at a chart portraying the earnings of Hey Wow Electronics Corporation. The chart, especially prepared for Hey Wow's annual report, depicts unmitigated glory in four delicious colors. That upward-sloping line, so thick, so solid, so thoroughly *established*, looks as though it will never quit. Nothing can break it. It can be bent, but only slightly. It looks as though it will go up and up forever!

But don't you bet on it.

MINOR AXIOM VII.
Beware the Correlation and Causality Delusions.

There is an old story about a fellow who stands on a street corner every day waving his arms and uttering strange cries. A cop goes up to him one day and asks what it's all about. "I'm keeping giraffes away," the fellow explains. "But we've never had any giraffes around here," says the cop. "Doing a good job, ain't I?" says the fellow.

It is characteristic of even the most rational minds to perceive links of cause and effect where none exist. When we have to, we invent them.

The human mind is an order-seeking organ. It is uncomfortable with chaos and will retreat from reality into fantasy if that is the only way it can sort things out to its satisfaction. Thus, when two or more events occur in close proximity, we insist on constructing elaborate causal links between them because that makes us comfortable.

It can also make us vulnerable, but we don't usually think of that until it is too late.

I'll give you a personal example. Many years ago, before Frank Henry and I had talked much about the Zurich Axioms, I made a little money jumping back and forth between IBM and Honeywell stock. Honeywell in those days was heavily committed to building big, general-purpose computers and was a direct competitor of IBM to a much greater extent than is true today. Over a period of eighteen months or so, I noticed that the two stocks' prices often moved in opposite directions. When Honeywell climbed for a few weeks, IBM would be drooping, and vice versa. I put a little money into what I thought was a very smart parlay: ride Honeywell up a way, jump off, buy IBM at a low point, ride *that* up . . . and so on.

It worked tolerably well a couple of times. I should have realized it was working only because I was lucky, but I wasn't that smart in those days. I thought it was working because . . . because . . . well, I constructed a causal relationship to fit the phenomenon I had been witnessing.

I theorized that there were a lot of big investors—mutual funds, insurance companies, and wealthy private plungers —who periodically shifted enormous mountains of cash from IBM to Honeywell and back. When Honeywell announced an attractive new product or made some other good move, all those hypothetical fat cats would sell off IBM stock in order to load themselves up with Honeywell—and vice versa. This rigged-up hypothesis, if true, would explain the opposite motions of the two stocks' prices.

Was it true? Almost certainly not. The truth undoubtedly was that the seemingly orderly price movements had been caused by events that coincided by pure chance. These events were random and unpredictable. The fact that those opposite price moves had occurred a few times in the past was no indication, and should never have been taken as an indication, that they would recur in the future. But my rigged-up causal relationship made the whole minuet seem more orderly than it was, and I confidently bet too much money on it.

I bought a bunch of Honeywell at what I thought was a low point. Whereupon Honeywell and IBM both plunged together like a pair of ducks with their tails shot off. Before I understood what was happening and abandoned my illusion of order, I had lost about 25 percent of my investment.

Unless you can actually see a cause operating, really *see* it, regard all causal hypotheses with the greatest skepticism. When you observe events happening together or in tandem, assume that the proximity results from chance factors unless you have hard evidence to the contrary. Always remember that you are dealing with chaos and conduct your affairs accordingly. As the Axiom says, chaos is not dangerous until it begins to look orderly.

Because so many people in the money world are so desperately seeking orderly patterns, places like Wall Street generate steady streams of ideas about possible causal links between this and that. Some of these postulated links seem plausible to many, others only to a few. But all of them have some kind of allure for that order-loving organ the human mind, and every one of them probably has meant trouble for somebody.

For example, one set of perceived links—laughed at by some, taken seriously by others—has to do with a phenomenon known as the Republican First-Year Jinx. Since the early decades of this century, the stock market has consistently slumped in the first year of every term served by a Republican President—first terms and second terms alike. It happened to Herbert Hoover once, Dwight Eisenhower twice, Richard Nixon twice, and Ronald Reagan (as of this writing) once. It even happened in the first twelve months of Gerald Ford's irregular three-year term.

The first question is: Why? And the second question is: What should an investor do about it, if anything?

The most likely answer to the first question is that the phenomenon has been caused by random events having nothing to do with the political party of the newly inaugurated President. Chance correlations with market movements are a dime a dozen, and this is one of them. It is like the Super Bowl Omen—the peculiar fact, often noted around Wall Street, that the market invariably rises in any year when January's Super Bowl game is won by a team tracing its origins back to the old National Football League. The Super Bowl Omen is great fun to talk about, but nobody seriously thinks a causal relationship exists between the football game and the stock market. The correlation just *happens*, that's all. And so it is with the Republican First-Year Jinx.

As for the second question—what to do about the jinx—the indicated answer is nothing.

But there are investors who insist on making something orderly out of it. Their theory is that the President's Republicanness *causes* the market to dip in his first year in office. Causes it how? Well, you can take your pick of hypotheses. One notion is that the Republican Party, billing itself as the party of business prosperity, raises people's financial expectations to an unrealistically high level. When they don't get rich instantly on Inauguration Day, they get disgruntled, and the backwash of disappointment swamps the stock market.

That is one theory. There are others. There is no need to waste our time on them, for none should be taken seriously. All are examples of the way in which people rig up phantom causal links to explain observed phenomena. And all are examples of the way in which a causal link, once invented and accepted, can make a phenomenon look more orderly than it probably is.

Which can be dangerous, as we've seen. If you believe the President's GOP-ness causes the stock market to slump, then you perceive an orderly series of events and may feel pushed to take action on them. You become like Professor Fisher, seeing patterns that aren't really there.

Maybe the Republican Jinx will operate true to form in the future, and maybe it won't. It began by chance and one day will end by chance. No predictions can be made about it one way or the other. It is, in fact, only another part of the chaos.

Guard against imagining causes when you can't actually observe them at work, and you will save yourself a lot of grief. Have fun at the Super Bowl game—but if the wrong team wins, see your bartender, not your broker.

MINOR AXIOM VIII.
Beware the Gambler's Fallacy.

Says the gambler: "I'm hot tonight!" Says the lottery-ticket buyer: "This is my lucky day!" Both are working themselves into a state of expectant euphoria in which they will put money at risk with less than their normal prudence. Both are likely to be sorry.

The Gambler's Fallacy is a peculiar variety of orderly illusion. In this case the perceived order is not in the chaotic world all around, but inside, in the self. When you say you are "hot," or you get the feeling that today is your lucky day, what you mean is that you are temporarily in a state in which random events will be influenced in your favor. In a disorderly world, with events whirling wildly around in all directions, you are a calm island of order. Events in your vicinity will stop the horse-play and obediently march to your tune. Roulette wheels and slot machines will click into place for you. Cards will fall your way. Horses will run their hearts out for you. Any lottery ticket you buy will be a winner. Should you decide to play the stock market and select an investment by jabbing a knifepoint into a newspaper while blindfolded, your stock will double by next week. You can't lose!

Like hell you can't.

It is surprising how many smart people allow themselves to be fooled by the Gambler's Fallacy. It shows up wherever money is wagered but is particularly prevalent around gambling casinos (hence its name). One of the most often-heard bits of useless advice at Las Vegas and Atlantic City is that you should "test" your luck every night before doing any serious betting. Indeed, some otherwise practical textbooks on gambling solemnly suggest this. The idea is that you place a few small bets at first—drop a couple of bucks into a slot machine, for instance—to see how your luck is running. If the machine swallows your offering without even saying thanks, you figure the deck of fate is stacked against you that night, so you might as well go back to your hotel room and watch TV. But if the machine returns your offering with interest, then you are ready for the big-time dice tables or the wheel.

All kinds of people believe in this illusion of order. The high rollers believe in it and so do the nickel-and-dimers. The rich who come to the casinos in furs and Ferraris believe in it, and so do those who will barely be able to afford a bus ticket home if they lose. It might be that all of us believe in it for some part of our lives.

Like many of these illusions, the Gambler's Fallacy has a lot of appeal. It *seems* true. In its cockeyed way, it has a rational sound.

Everybody can recall episodes from his or her own experience that seem to support it. If you play bridge, poker, or Monopoly with any regularity, you are keenly aware that there are some nights when the cards or dice are so good to you that it is embarrassing, and then there are other nights when you wish you'd stayed home with a good book. There are nights when you are hot and nights when you are not.

And the phenomenon is not restricted to the gaming table but extends into all activities of your life. There are days when all your decisions turn out brilliantly right, everybody smiles at you, unexpected checks arrive in the mail, and your rival at the office decides to go off and seek her fortune in Australia. And there are other days when everything you touch turns to dust and ashes.

How natural to see some kind of order-making mechanism behind all this.

The illusion is reinforced by the stories gamblers love to tell: amazing stories of "hot" states and runs of unbeatable luck. You hear those stories around every casino and every newsstand where lottery tickets are sold. Some are only locally famous, but some are international classics.

For example, there is the incredible tale of Charles Wells, who became immortalized in a popular song of the Gay Nineties, "The Man Who Broke the Bank at Monte Carlo." Wells accomplished this legendary feat not once but on three separate nights in 1891.

"Breaking the bank" was not quite as dramatic as it sounded. It didn't mean you bankrupted the casino. All it meant was that you exhausted the supply of house playing money allotted to a table. Still, it happened so rarely that it was front-page news when somebody managed to do it even once. (The casino cooperated happily in the publicity by ceremoniously draping the "broken" table with a black cloth. The news could be counted on to lure in a lot of new suckers and their money on the following night.)

Wells's game was roulette. The last of his three winning nights was the most astounding of all. On that night he chose to play single numbers. This is roulette's longest shot. You pick any of the numbers from 1 to 36 and put your money on it. If you win, the payoff is $36 for every $1 you bet. On the old-style Monte Carlo wheel, the odds against you were 37 to 1.

Wells put his money on 5 and left it there to ripen. The number 5 came up five times in a row. The table was busted. Wells walked out of the casino with somewhat more than 100,000 French francs, the spending power of which in those days equaled more than a million of today's dollars.

Then there was Caroline ("La Belle") Otero, perhaps the most famous and some say the most beautiful of the celebrated courtesans who flourished around Monte Carlo in its days of glory. She was brought to the fabled gambling resort at age eighteen by a man who was evidently both an inept gambler and a scoundrel. He lost his wad at the tables and abandoned her. She was down to her last two louis—20-franc pieces, each worth perhaps $100 in today's currency. On a desperate impulse, she went to a roulette table and bet those two louis on red.

The color wager—red or black—is one of roulette's even-money or coin-toss bets. If you win, you double your money. Caroline Otero was too frightened to watch the outcome, so she walked away from the table, simply leaving her money to fatten or vanish as the case might be.

Red came up twenty-eight times in a row. The bank was broken, and the abandoned girl, suddenly rich, was transformed instantly into Monte Carlo's acknowledged queen.

Stories like that are good fun. They and others like them were cited in the nineteenth century and are still cited today in support of the Gambler's Fallacy. "You see there *are* times when people get hot!" a believer will say. "These stories prove it—all you have to do is wait till you're hot, then play like mad!"

They prove nothing of the kind. All they prove, in fact, is that winning streaks happen.

Toss a coin enough times, and sooner or later you are going to have a long run of heads. But there is nothing orderly about this run. You cannot know in advance when it will start. And when it has started, you cannot know how long it will continue.

And so it is with roulette, the horses, the art market, or any other game in which you put money at risk. If you play long enough, you will enjoy winning streaks—perhaps some memorable ones, with which you will undoubtedly bore your friends for the rest of your life. But there is no orderly way in which you can cash in on these streaks. You can't see them coming, and you can't predict their duration. They are merely one more part of the chaos.

If you are betting on red at a roulette wheel and red comes up three times in a row, that is nice. But what does it tell you about the future? Are you in on the beginning of a run of twenty-eight? Are you hot? Should you increase the size of your bet?

Many would. Which is one reason why many walk out of casinos with nothing but holes in their pockets.

As we learned in our studies of the Second Axiom, countless speculators and gamblers have been bankrupted by failing to quit while they were ahead. The Gambler's Fallacy tends to encourage that failure, for it engenders the feeling that one is temporarily invincible.

That is a dangerous feeling to have. Nobody is invincible, not even for half a second.

Caroline Otero and Charles Wells were lucky. They had to stop playing because the house ran out of money—and in any case, some of their own money was removed from play after each coup because of house limits on the sizes of permissible bets. They were saved by these circumstances. If the facts had been otherwise and they had continued to play, sooner or later both would have lost, and we would not know their names today.

They were not invincible. Both seemed to have the feeling that they were. Perhaps their good judgment was addled by those remarkable winning streaks. It might be hard, indeed, to remain perfectly rational after an experience like that. At any rate, Caroline Otero and Charles Wells, in their subsequent lives, acted as though they were afflicted with two unusually grandiose cases of the Gambler's Fallacy.

Both took a lot of long-shot chances, as though airily assuming they would stay hot forever.

They didn't. Caroline Otero died broke in a seedy Paris apartment. Charles Wells died broke in jail.

Speculative Strategy

Now let's see specifically how the Fifth Axiom advises you to handle your money.

The Axiom warns you not to see order where order does not exist. This doesn't mean you should despair of ever finding an advantageous bet or a promising investment. On the contrary, you should study the speculative medium in which you are interested—the poker table, the art world, whatever it is—and when you see something that looks good, take your best shot.

But don't be hypnotized by an illusion of order. Your studying may have improved the odds in your favor, but you still cannot ignore the overwhelmingly large role of chance in the venture. It is unlikely that your studying has created a sure thing for you, or even a nearly sure thing. You are still dealing with chaos. As long as you remain keenly alert to that fact, you can keep yourself from getting hurt.

Your internal monologue should go like this: "Okay, I've done my homework as well as I know how. I think this bet can pay off for me. But since I cannot see or control all the random events that will affect what happens to my money, I know that the chance of my being wrong is large. Therefore I will stay light on my feet, ready to jump this way or that when whatever is going to happen happens."

And that is the lesson of the Fifth Axiom. You are getting to be a smarter speculator all the time.

The Sixth Major Axiom:
ON MOBILITY

Avoid putting down roots. They impede motion.

In the lexicon of modern mental-health theory, rootlessness is in the same category as worry. Both are felt to be bad for you.

It is certainly nice in many ways to have roots. To feel you belong in some familiar place amid old friends and good neighbors: this can bring a glow to the heart. The opposites of this cozy situation—rootlessness, a state of drifting, alienation —seem cold and uncomfortable by comparison. Undoubtedly that is why most shrinks believe we ought to have roots.

But you should approach this roots business warily. If you let it impinge on your financial life, it can cost you a lot of money. The more earnestly you seek that feeling of being surrounded by the old, the familiar, and the comfortable, the less successful you are likely to be as a speculator.

The Axiom doesn't refer only to geographic mobility or the lack of it—the old-hometown kind of rootedness. That is part of it for many middle-class people, especially those trying to make a buck in the real estate game. But it is only a part. What the Axiom means more than anything else is a state of mind, a way of thinking, a habitual method of organizing your life.

The message comes in two halves, each covered by a minor axiom.

MINOR AXIOM IX.
Do not become trapped in a souring venture because of sentiments like loyalty and nostalgia.

Let's look at the real estate business first. A New Jersey realtor, Janice Shattuck, tells a sad story of opportunity missed because of roots.

A couple in early middle age had lived in the same house for two decades. The twenty-year mortgage was paid off, and now every nickel of the home's capital value was theirs free and clear. This lump of capital was their biggest asset, as is true of many middle-income people. With their children grown and gone and expenses diminished, they were in a position to put that capital to work in some serious speculation. With luck, they could sail into old age rich.

Janice Shattuck, a personal friend, told them she thought selling their home would be a good idea. The street on which they lived was showing signs of an economic decline. Because of random circumstances, several houses were in disrepair. Two were owned by absentee landlords and rented to groups of young people attending a nearby college—not the best guarantee of efficient home maintenance. The street was beginning to have a tired, shabby look.

Mrs. Shattuck was even able to tell her friends she thought she could produce a buyer for them. One of the absentee landlords was thinking about extending his empire and had long had an eye on their house, a big rambling structure well suited to use as a college dormitory. Mrs. Shattuck believed he would offer a fair price. She urged her friends to take it while they could get it.

But they couldn't bring themselves to sell. They had roots here, they explained. This was where they had brought up their family. The big old house was full of memories. They couldn't bear to think of it in use as a college dorm. Moreover, some of the older neighbors were urging them not to sell. To allow one more house to be converted into a dorm, to move away and leave all the problems with those who remained—this seemed unneighborly and disloyal.

And so Mrs. Shattuck's friends stayed. The neighborhood continued to decline. Other houses were sold to less careful owners— including houses belonging to the very folks who had talked most earnestly about loyalty. Mrs. Shattuck's friends finally put their house on the market. So far, no buyer has appeared. When one does, the offered price is going to be drastically lower than they could have secured when they were first urged to sell. The longer they have to wait, the lower the price is likely to go.

There are times when you have to choose between roots and money. If you are interested in money—which is presumably why you are studying speculation—it is a mistake to let yourself get too attached to any physical thing in which your capital is invested. Get attached to people, but not to houses or neighborhoods.

Not to companies, either. You never know when it may be wise to sell out. Be sure you don't let roots impede you.

Frank Henry knew a man who worked as chief engineer of a small manufacturing company. Over the years he had accumulated a big amount of the company's common and preferred stock. There had been a time when the company was prosperous and the stock price high, but that time had not lasted long. The company was now in serious trouble because of changes in its markets—particularly the arrival of some merciless Japanese competitors.

The general facts of this trouble were public knowledge, and the stock price was sagging badly. The engineer believed, however, that the problems were even worse than anybody guessed. Comparing his company's products with the Japanese competition, he found a substantial difference in quality. The Japanese products, though priced lower, were superior. The engineer saw no way in which his company's double disadvantage could be overcome. Sooner or later, he was convinced, the competition would drive the company to its death.

He should have sold out, but roots impeded him.

He harbored confused feelings of loyalty to the little company. These feelings were heightened by a lot of don't-give-up-the-ship speeches by the board chairman and chief executive officer, the major stockholder. The chairman, an incurable optimist, loudly proclaimed the fact that he was continuing to buy *more* of the stock for his personal portfolio. He believed it was important to do this. Since SEC and stock-exchange rules required him to make public the extent of his interest in the company, any sell-off by him would have become known. That would have been hurtful publicity. His theory was that he could generate good publicity by doing the opposite. In buying more stock, he felt, he was demonstrating faith in the company's viability and future prospects. He was showing loyalty.

The engineer doubted that the chairman's gesture was having any notable effect. The common and preferred stock prices were leapfrogging past each other in their steady progress downhill. Shareholders' and employees' morale was low and falling lower. It was time to get out. But the engineer couldn't make himself get—and one of the main reasons was the chairman's gesture of loyalty.

If one investor is a net buyer of a security while another is a net seller, then in effect one is buying from the other. The transactions are, of course, handled through dealers or brokers and specialists on an exchange trading floor, but the effect of matching up a buyer and a seller is the same as though it were a face-to-face deal. The engineer had the uncomfortable awareness, therefore, that when he put his shares up for sale, they would be bought from him by the chairman.

The engineer would end sold out, while the chairman would end with a fat portfolio of a stock that might soon be worthless. It didn't seem right, somehow.

And so the engineer sat tight. In time, he and the chairman both ended with portfolios of worthless stock.

Many years later, Frank Henry was involved in an unrelated business deal that brought him into brief contact with the former board chairman, now the owner of an expanding chain of stores. The man seemed prosperous and content. He talked happily of some recent stock market successes. He had made some money by selling stocks short in a falling market. He was obviously familiar with the technique of shorting, in which you sell a stock before you own it, hoping the price will fall. If it does fall, you fulfill the sale by buying the stock for less money than you've received.

As the former board chairman talked about this, a small but wicked thought began to germinate in Frank Henry's mind.

He wondered if the chairman had been as optimistic about that troubled little company as he had pretended. Perhaps, Frank Henry surmised, the man had maintained two brokerage accounts, as many big wheeler-dealers do: an openly declared one and a secret one. While loudly and proudly buying the company's stock in one account, maybe he had been shorting it in the other.

It was just a thought.

MINOR AXIOM X.
Never hesitate to abandon a venture if something more attractive comes into view.

There are many ways in which you can get rooted in a speculative medium, to the detriment of your overriding goal of making money. One of the most common—it sneaks up and takes people by surprise—is to get into a situation in which you aren't sure whether you are conducting a speculation or a hobby.

You have a collection of rare coins or stamps, let's say. Or you have a living room that has turned into an art museum. You have reached a preset goal of doubling your money, but now you can't bring yourself to sell the stuff. You've become too attached to it—or maybe some artsy-craftsy type has started you thinking it's wrong to speculate in art for money. So there your collection sits at home, its capital value trapped within it. Meanwhile some other good speculations have come into view —speculations in which you could put that capital to good use. You have a hunch about the price of silver, maybe. Or you have a chance to get in on some local real estate speculation that looks good to you. What are you going to do?

You've got to decide whether you are a speculator or not.

Never get attached to things, only to people. Getting attached to things decreases your mobility, the capacity to move fast when the need arises. Once you get yourself rooted, your efficiency as a speculator goes down markedly.

Another common way to get rooted is to get into a situation in which you are waiting for something to pay off. This may happen to even more people than the speculation/hobby dilemma. It is possible to get trapped in a waiting game for years, while dozens of other good speculative opportunities drift tantalizingly within reach of your fingers, which are powerless to grasp them.

You've bought $10,000 worth of Hoo Boy Computer, we'll say. You're aiming at an ending position of $15,000. But Hoo Boy turns out to be a dog. It goes neither up nor down. Year after year the mangy old hound just sits there with its tongue lolling out.

Meanwhile your eye is attracted by Hey Wow Electronics. Some piece of hard news makes you think Hey Wow is more likely to score a big gain in the next year or so than Hoo Boy Computer. You would buy a bundle of Hey Wow if you had any capital, but you don't have a free nickel. It's all tied up in Hoo Boy.

What do you do? The common reaction is to go on sitting on that Hoo Boy stock. "I can't sell now! I've got to wait for my payoff!"

But think. If you have a good reason to believe a faster payoff is possible in Hey Wow, why *not* make the switch? It's the same money no matter where it's invested. If it grows to $15,000 in Hey Wow instead of Hoo Boy, you'll have just as much fun celebrating.

Never get rooted in an investment because of the feeling that it "owes" you something—or, just as bad, the feeling that you "owe" it enough time to show what it can do. If it isn't going anywhere and you see something better, change trains.

The only thing you lose by changing instead of staying is the dealer's or broker's commission. If the capital value of the original investment has changed during the time you've held it, the act of selling makes you liable for a capital gains tax—or, conversely, wins you the right to declare a capital loss. But since we are talking about selling something that hasn't gone anywhere in particular, this consideration is likely to be minor.

Of course, there is the possibility of regret, which we've

studied under other Axioms. If you switch from Hoo Boy into Hey Wow, you are going to experience several different kinds of unpleasant emotions if Hoo Boy, that tired old hound, suddenly perks up and goes bounding uphill. That can happen, of course.

But the possibility of regret will also exist if you *don't* switch. While you are still patiently sitting on Hoo Boy, Hey Wow may suddenly come to life, just as you suspected it might. You will then wish to kick yourself for staying with your original investment.

Since the possibility of regret is the same no matter what you do, you might as well leave it out of the calculation. It is self-canceling. The decision to stay or switch should ride solely on the question of which speculation, in your judgment, seems to offer the best promise for a speedy payoff.

This is the question you should ask yourself whenever you are holding one investment but are attracted to another. Don't get rooted, whether because of a speculation/hobby dilemma, a waiting-for-a-payoff hangup, or—just as much of a problem for some—fears and worries about abandoning something familiar for something new and unknown. Determine where your best chance seems to lie—and go for it.

Speculative Strategy

The Sixth Axiom urges you to preserve your mobility. It warns against the many things that can get you rooted, to the detriment of your speculative career: sentiments like loyalty, hangups like the wish to wait around for a payoff. It says you must stay footloose, ready to jump away from trouble or seize opportunities quickly.

This doesn't mean you have to bounce from one speculation to another like a Ping-Pong ball. All your moves should be made only after careful assessment of the odds for and against, and no move should be made for trivial reasons. But when a venture is clearly souring, or when something clearly more promising comes into view, then you must sever those roots and go.

Be careful. Don't let those roots grow too thick to cut.

The Seventh Major Axiom:
ON INTUITION

A hunch can be trusted if it can be
explained.

A hunch is a piece of feeling-stuff. It is a mysterious little clump
of not-quite-knowledge: a mental event that feels something
like knowledge but doesn't feel perfectly trustworthy. As a
speculator you are likely to be hit by hunches frequently. Some
will be strong and insistent. What should you do about them?

Learn to use them, if you can.

That is easy advice to give but, as you will undoubtedly discover, not so easy to carry out. The subject of intuition is complicated, imperfectly understood, and troublesome to many
people. There are three distinct approaches to the phenomenon:

Scorn. Many investor/speculators studiously ignore their own
hunches and laugh at other people's. They insist on backing all
speculative moves with facts and factlike material. It is often
pretty goofy material—charts, economists' forecasts—but to
people in this group, it seems more trustworthy than hunches.
They will often make a move even when their intuition is telling them strongly that the move is wrong. "The chart says it's
right, and that's what I go by."

Indiscriminate trust. Then there are people who lean on
hunches too hard, too often, and without enough skepticism.

Any wayward intuition becomes a reason for making a move, even when a rational analysis of the situation might yield completely different ideas. "I go with my hunches," these people will say proudly, neglecting to add that those wonderful hunches have quite often led to speculative calamities.

Discriminating use. This is the Zurich approach. The thought behind it is that intuition *can* be useful. It seems a shame to scorn such a potentially valuable speculative tool in a categorical way—to throw out all hunches just because some are silly. On the other hand, it is true that some hunches deserve to be tossed in the garbage can. The challenge is to discern which are worthy of your attention and which are not.

So the first step is to find out just what a hunch *is*. Where does this odd little piece of nearly-knowledge come from?

It turns out to be less mysterious than it seems. There are some who would explain intuition by talking about extrasensory perception or occult powers, but none of that is necessary. A hunch is a perfectly ordinary mental event. When you are hit with a strong hunch—"I think that company is in worse trouble than they're letting on"—the possibility is that this conclusion is based on actual, solid information that is stored somewhere in your mind. What makes it perplexing is that it is *information you don't know you possess.*

Is that plausible? Of course. It is an everyday mental occurrence. Dr. Eugene Gendlin, A University of Chicago psychologist who has spent years studying this subject, points out that it is a common human experience to know something without knowing how you know it.

Dr. Gendlin points out that you take in colossal amounts of data every day—vastly more than you can store in your conscious mind and recall in the form of discrete data bits. Most of it is stored in some other reservoir just below or behind the conscious level.

For instance, think of a certain man or woman who has played a significant role in your life. This person doesn't come to you in discrete data bits—brown hair, blue eyes, likes Chinese food, and so on. There are millions of such data bits that you have stored over the years, far more than you could list in your lifetime. Instead of coming to you in bits, the person comes *whole*. Everything you know and feel about him or her, everything you have ever thought, felt, or experienced in connection with this person—it all comes at once, mysteriously pulled up from that colossal library of not-quite-knowing.

Imagine meeting this man or woman in the street. You instantly know who it is. With no conscious thinking at all you instantly react in appropriate ways. Yet if I were to ask you *how* you recognize this person, precisely what your clues are—the shape of the nose? the manner of walking?—you would have no answer to give. You *know* you know your friend, but you don't know how you know.

Similarly, if this man or woman telephones you, you instantly recognize the voice. How? By precisely what clues? There is no answer. If you were to attempt to describe that voice to me so that I, too, could recognize it, you would find the task impossible. The information is in your head somewhere, but you don't know just what it is or where it is.

This is the stuff hunches are made of. A good hunch is something that you know, but you don't know how you know it.

For instance, a woman who speculates in New England real estate told me about a hunch that visited her in the middle of the night. She had renovated a very old seashore house in Maine and had been trying to sell it but had not heard any offers that came close enough to her asking price. One offer was almost acceptable but was just shy of her preplanned ending position. She was holding for more and feeling fairly confident.

Then, in the small quiet hours before a rainy dawn, she came suddenly wide awake and found herself gripped by a powerful, insistent hunch that she ought to take that offer. The intuition said that the market for old Maine coast homes was about to soften, maybe collapse. She didn't know how she knew this. She just *knew*.

But she was afraid to trust the hunch. She was perplexed by the usual problem: She couldn't see the library of information on which the hunch was based.

She and I talked about it. Her first inclination was to laugh at the hunch and hope it would go away. But then we began to come around to the view that it might well be based on solid, trustworthy information.

She had long made it her business, after all, to study the economy of the Maine coast as it impinged on real estate. She subscribed to a couple of local newspapers, belonged to a property owners' association, talked frequently with realtors and other knowledgeable folk. She also kept herself well informed on national and world events. She was a *Business Week* reader, among other things. Thus it could be said with perfect confidence that she possessed a big store of data relevant to the selling price of a house on the Maine coast.

Much of this information was stored, however, on a not quite-conscious level of her mind. Indeed, probably most of it was. The fully conscious part was like the visible tip of an iceberg.

The troublesome hunch had arisen, we concluded, when connections were made in that huge nonconscious data bank. Facts had drifted together like pieces of a jigsaw puzzle, without her conscious direction. Perhaps there were scores of these little bits of forgotten data: something she had read, something she had overheard at a meeting, a remark made months ago by a realtor. Put together, they resulted in an intuitive conviction that the Maine coast real estate market was riding for a fall.

She decided to trust the hunch. She accepted the highest offer for her house. Only a month or so later it was apparent that she had made a brilliantly right move. The offer she had taken was the highest she was likely to have seen for a long, long time.

We are now in a position to understand what the Seventh Axiom means when it says, "A hunch can be trusted if it can be explained."

When a hunch hits you, the first thing to do is ask whether a big enough library of data could exist in your mind to have generated that hunch. Though you don't know and can't know precisely what the relevant data bits might be, is it plausible to think they exist?

If it's a hunch about Maine coast real estate, ask whether you are genuinely knowledgeable on this particular topic. Have you studied it? Have you been following its ups and downs? If it's a hunch about the price of silver, have you absorbed a lot of knowledge about the metal and its complex interrelationships with other economic goings-on? If it's a hunch about a person —"this guy is out to cheat me"—have you known him well enough and long enough to make character insights possible?

The reason for subjecting hunches to this rigorous testing is that sometimes we get flashes of intuition that aren't based on good, hard fact. They are airy nothings. Where do they come from? Search me. They are like dreams. They come out of nowhere, they mean nothing, they lead nowhere. They are simply the brain playing with itself.

You're reading the paper one morning and come across a little article about the installation of a new president at Hoo Boy Computer. Suddenly you've got this terrific hunch. The new man is going to take Hoo Boy to magnificent new heights. He'll gobble up the market! He'll send IBM reeling! The stock price will soar like a rocket!

But before you call your broker, put this wonderful hunch to the test. Your internal monologue might go something like this:

"Okay, friend, let's look at this calmly. What do you know about Hoo Boy Computer?"

"Well, uh, once in a while I read something about it. Sounds like a good solid outfit."

"But have you made a special study of it? Really followed its fortunes?"

"No, can't say I have."

"And how about this new president? Know a lot about him, do you?"

"Uh, not exactly."

"Matter of fact, you never heard of him before, right? So what gives you this great feeling of faith in him?"

"Well, the newspaper reporter seemed to think he was a sound man."

"The reporter probably never heard of him before either. Probably half the stuff in that article came right out of a company press release. So you really think you've got enough of a data base to generate a reliable hunch?"

"Well, uh—"

"Come on, friend, let's go get some beer and forget it."

This kind of testing doesn't guarantee that you will never have an inaccurate hunch, of course. Even the most solid-based hunch can be wrong. Conversely, an out-of-nowhere hunch can be right, just as any wild guess can. What this procedure does do for you is to improve the odds in your favor. It puts you one up on those who scorn all intuition and also on those who think all hunches are sent from heaven. You are more likely to act on good hunches than the first group, more likely to discard bad ones than the second group.

Whatever you do, however, keep the rest of the Axioms about you. No matter how good a hunch feels, don't let it lull you into a state of overconfidence. Stay worried. Intuition can be a useful speculative tool, but it isn't the long-sought, infallible formula for 100 percent correct money decisions. As we have noted before, there is no such formula.

MINOR AXIOM XI.
Never confuse a hunch with a hope.

When you want something very much, you can all too easily talk yourself into believing it will happen. This fact of human psychology confounds little children dreaming of what they want for Christmas, and it confounds speculators dreaming of all the money they're going to make.

You visit a small-town art show and buy a couple of paintings by an obscure artist named Trashworthy. You get them home and discover that you don't like them quite as much as you thought you did. They are rather weird, in fact. A nasty little voice somewhere inside suggests that maybe you've wasted your money. But those whining words are quickly drowned out by the thunder of a mighty hunch. Someday, the hunch says, Trashworthy will get the recognition he deserves! Those paintings will be sought by collectors everywhere! Great museums will bid for them!

Is it a hunch worth listening to? Or only a hope?

My personal rule is to be highly skeptical anytime I have a hunch that something I want to happen will happen. This doesn't mean all such hunches are wrong. It means only that one should examine them with extra care and double one's guard in case of trouble.

By contrast, I'm much more inclined to trust an intuition pointing to some outcome I don't want. If I had bought those paintings and generated a hunch that Trashworthy was never going to make it (and if I had enough knowledge of art to make such a hunch plausible), my inclination would be to unload fast.

Speculative Strategy

The Seventh Axiom suggests that it is a mistake either to laugh at hunches categorically or to trust them indiscriminately. Though intuition is not infallible, it can be a useful speculative tool if handled with care and skepticism. There is nothing magical or otherworldly about intuition. It is simply a manifestation of a perfectly ordinary mental experience: that of knowing something without knowing how one knows it.

If you are hit by a strong hunch telling you to make a certain move with your money, the Axiom urges you to put it to a test. Trust it only if you can explain it—that is, only if you can identify within your mind a stored body of information out of which that hunch might reasonably be supposed to have arisen. If you have no such library of data, disregard the hunch.

The associated Minor Axiom xi warns, finally, that a hunch can easily be confused with a hope. Be especially wary of any intuitive flash that seems to promise some outcome you want badly.

The Eighth Major Axiom:
ON RELIGION AND THE OCCULT

It is unlikely that God's plan for the universe includes making you rich.

A Protestant minister used to come to our house for dinner once in a while when I was a youngster. He and Frank Henry had known each other as boys in the little town of Wädenswil, on the south shore of Lake Zurich. The minister had migrated to America as a young man and was now the pastor of a little church somewhere in New Jersey.

He was bubbling with enthusiasm one night. The Lord had given his church a great opportunity, he reported. A member of his flock, an elderly man, was about to move to a warmer climate. The move had to be accomplished fast for some reason or another, and the man wanted it to be a clean break, with no loose ends left behind. Among these loose ends was a holding of perhaps a dozen acres of undeveloped land at one edge of the town. He had bought this property many years back as an investment but had never done anything with it. He now wanted to sell it before he moved away. As a parting gift to the church, he was offering to sell it for exactly what he had paid years ago.

The minister was tremendously excited over this. His parish had never had much money. Here was a chance to make a killing overnight! Real estate values all over town had been soaring, and the area where the church member's property lay was considered particularly desirable for homesites. The church could either resell the land for an instant profit or wait a little longer, put in a road or two, and sell off quarter-acre lots individually for still more profit. At last, the minister exulted, the parish was going to have money for all the good work that needed to be done!

Frank Henry said he was happy to hear this good news. He added that it sounded as though it might be a little too good to be true. In his experience, he said, instant killings and sure things usually turned out to be traps. Amateur speculators were always falling into them and crawling back out with their pockets emptied.

The minister said pooh-pooh. This was a gift from God. Sometimes the Lord punishes us and sometimes He rewards us. It isn't our place to ask a lot of questions. We can only accept what is given. The minister wasn't worried.

Frank Henry and I heard the end of the story a long time later. At the minister's urging, the congregation voted to buy the departed member's property and set up a committee to study what to do with it. The committee determined that the best option would be to subdivide it and sell off individual lots. The committee chairman and the minister went to the town hall to apply for the necessary permits, and there they met the local building inspector, who told them the bad news.

That piece of land, he said, had some troublesome characteristics. It looked dry enough on the surface, but a couple of feet down it was pure swamp. No septic system you put in there would ever work right. More than one owner over the years had wanted to develop the place, but the town had always refused to allow it, unless the owner wanted to install a staggeringly expensive drainage system. That was why it had always remained undeveloped.

The church had been had.

The moral of the story, as Frank Henry put it, is that you can't pray yourself rich. Indeed, if money is on your mind while praying, you are more likely to pray yourself poor. If you depend on God or any other supernatural power or agency to bring you wealth, the chances are you will drop your guard and get flattened.

If there is a God, a question on which the Axioms hold no opinion, there is no evidence that this supreme being gives a hoot whether you die rich or poor. The Bible says several times, in fact, that from the viewpoint of maintaining a healthy Christian or Jewish soul, you are probably better off poor. Many eastern religions hold the same belief. (And Abraham Lincoln remarked once that God must have had a special love for the poor, since He made so many of them.) Thus, as far as the Axioms are concerned, it makes no difference whether you are devoutly religious, an atheist, or something in between. No matter what your beliefs might be, thoughts of God or other supernatural help should play no part in your speculative behavior.

Leaning on supernatural help produces the same result as leaning on a forecast or an illusion of order. It lulls you into a dangerously unworried state. Priests, ministers, and rabbis are always telling people they shouldn't pray for money, but many do. If it isn't a direct request for some specific financial outcome, it's a blithe assumption by many pious people that they are beneficiaries of some kind of heavenly purse insurance: "God will protect me."

Don't count on it. God may do much for you, but one thing He plainly isn't concerned about is the size of your bank account. That's your problem. Yours alone.

Jesse Livermore, whom we met in our studies of another Axiom, leaned not on God but on another kind of otherworldly help. This may have contributed heavily to the final downfall of this complicated man. His story is worth examining.

Born poor on a Massachusetts farm, Livermore determined early in life that he would like to be rich. He went to Boston in 1893 and got a job in a stockbrokerage firm. Electronic display devices had not yet been invented; instead, stock price quotations were chalked on huge blackboards by agile young clerks scurrying up and down ladders. This was Livermore's first job. As he matured in it, he developed what seemed to his friends an uncanny ability to guess which way prices were going to move.

The ability was undoubtedly a combination of good hunching and luck, but some began to mutter about clairvoyance and other occult powers. Livermore never totally accepted this as an explanation of his speculative success, but he never totally rejected it either. He went through his whole life wondering if it was true. Frank Henry, for one, believed Livermore would have been far better off if he had never been introduced to such mystical musings.

After he had been clerking for a few months, Livermore began to put money on his price predictions. The speculative medium he chose was a kind of betting parlor, common in Boston as in other cities, called a bucket shop.

Bucket shops promoted stock market gambling in its most bizarre and exaggerated forms. In a bucket shop you didn't buy stocks themselves. Instead you placed various kinds of bets on price movements. It was pure horserace. The odds were rigged in favor of the house. To win, a speculator needed not only a lot of luck and good hunches but also a firm command of other skills we've been studying: when to cut losses, how to establish an ending position, and so on.

Jesse Livermore found that he had these skills in abundance. He was a natural-born speculator. Starting with the tiniest of stakes—nickels and dimes saved out of his paltry salary—he quite quickly amassed something like $2,500, an enormous amount for a young man in those days. He sharpened his skills to such a degree that one bucket shop after another told him to take his money somewhere else.

He took it to Wall Street: the big time. There he quickly established himself as one of the cleverest speculators who ever hit the Street. He was famous before he reached the age of thirty.

With his flowing blond hair and icy blue eyes, Jesse Livermore attracted women and newspaper reporters wherever he went. He married three times and kept mistresses in apartments and hotels all over America and Europe. He traveled with a herd of flunkies and sycophants. He could hardly walk a block in New York without being buttonholed by somebody who wanted investment advice. He photographed well and interviewed well; he looked and sounded like a man of unshakable confidence. But inside, he was constantly being gnawed by that question about clairvoyance.

He didn't know if he was clairvoyant or not. A lot of breathless newspaper and magazine articles said he was, and the sycophants all chorused agreement. Livermore thought sometimes that it might be so. At other times he concluded that the whole idea was nonsense.

He did have some astounding strokes of luck, which gave support to the notion that he could see the future. He strolled into a broker's office one day in 1906 and said he wanted to sell Union Pacific short. The broker was perplexed. Sell *Union Pacific* short? It was a supremely foolhardy thing to do. A bull market was in progress. Union Pacific was one of the hottest growth stocks on the board. Far from selling it short, the great majority of speculators were greedily buying it on margin.

But Livermore insisted on going short. The only explanation he ever offered was that he had a hunch the price was too high and a "correction" was coming. On the following day he returned to the broker's office and sold another large bundle of the giant railroad company's shares short.

The day after that, April 18, 1906, San Francisco was devastated by an earthquake. Millions of dollars in Union Pacific track and other property, plus untold millions in potential earnings, vanished beneath the rubble. The company's stock price dropped like a stone. Jesse Livermore came out of the experience some $300,000 richer.

Seemingly weird events like that are bound to happen to anybody who speculates long enough. Every risk-taker has similar tales to tell. They will almost certainly happen to you. They don't "prove" anything except that random events crash around blindly, hurting some, enriching others, and not caring which is which. Jesse Livermore undoubtedly was not the only plunger who sold Union Pacific short before the San Francisco earthquake, or who profited in some way or another from the great catastrophe. It isn't likely that many of the others thought they possessed a magical power to see the future. They must have realized they were just lucky. Livermore, too, was just lucky. But the "clairvoyant" label had been attached to him, and the Union Pacific episode made it stick all the tighter.

There were times in his life when he tried earnestly to shake it off. This usually happened when his luck or "clairvoyance" forsook him, which luck will always do in time. When he was broke or going broke, he seemed to realize he had been depending too heavily on the supposed ability to see the future, and then he would try to convince himself and others that he really had a more solid speculative footing than clairvoyance.

This happened for the last time in 1940. He had been bankrupt in 1934, had built up a new fortune, but once again was in the process of losing it. In an apparent attempt to demonstrate that he was speculating by means of a rational system, rather than magic, he wrote a peculiar little book, published in 1940, entitled *How to Trade in Stocks—the Livermore Formula for Combining Time Element and Price.*

It was the kind of book that would have been applauded by Professor Irving Fisher, the fellow who went down the tubes in 1929 because he thought he saw patterns in the stock market. The book was a hymn to patterns. It contained charts and instructions about "Pivotal Points" and "Secondary Reactions" and things like that.

It was perfect nonsense. Anybody who attempted to beat the market by following these instructions would end up very confused and perhaps broke—unless, of course, he or she was lucky. The book proved nothing except Livermore's intense desire, at that point in his life, to get as far from the clairvoyant question as he could.

Perhaps he tried, in the end, to invent a speculative system that mixed charting and clairvoyance. That may have worked even worse than when he leaned on either one separately. One afternoon in December 1940, Jesse Livermore walked into New York's Sherry-Netherland Hotel, drank two old-fashioneds, went to the men's room, and shot himself dead.

Of course it is never possible to know exactly why somebody has chosen to end his or her life. Even when the person leaves a note, which Livermore didn't, we are always left wondering which are real reasons and which are just easy explanations. Jesse Lauriston Livermore was a complicated man with a complicated life, and it is conceivable his suicide was prompted by problems we know nothing of. "There were twenty different Livermores," Frank Henry said sadly. "I only knew one of him."

Still, it does seem likely that speculative difficulties were in the bag of trouble that weighed the man down. Speculation had been the great obsession of his life. At the time he was drinking his last two old-fashioneds at the Sherry-Netherland, his financial affairs were in disarray for the fourth time in his life. For the fourth time he was facing a painful truth: His approach to speculation was decidedly fallible. The voyance was not half as clair as he could have hoped. If he was leaning on that supposed gift of prophecy, it had let him down.

None of this means you are in danger of coming to Jesse Livermore's tragic end. The Livermore story is only an unusually bizarre illustration of the way in which occult beliefs can get in the way of sound speculative thinking. Leaning on such beliefs may not be hazardous to your health, but it is to your money.

MINOR AXIOM XII.
If astrology worked, all astrologers would be rich.

This minor axiom seems to pick on astrology, but that is only because, in America and the rest of the western world, astrology is the most popular of occult beliefs. A recent Gallup survey showed that 32 million American adults believe in astrology, while at least that many more are occasional readers of newspaper and magazine horoscopes. Other occult disciplines such as witchcraft and the Tarot claim fewer adherents, but Minor Axiom xii is addressed to them as much as to the stargazers.

The thought offered for your consideration is this. If you are attracted by astrology or some other mystical or supernatural doctrine, by all means enter into its substance and spirit as deeply as pleases you. Play with it, make it a part of your life—do what you wish with it. But before you try to use it to help you make money, do yourself a favor. Look around at the practitioners of this doctrine—and particularly at those who profess to be its teachers, priests and gurus—and ask one question: *Are they rich?*

If they are no richer than any other random group of men

and women, then you have learned a useful fact. No matter what this occult doctrine might do for you in terms of inner peace and all that, one thing it won't do is fatten your bank account.

As you will discover, astrologers and astrology believers are no richer as a group than anybody else. Nor are believers in Tarot cards, psychic powers, or any other mystical, pseudoscientific, or religious system. When it comes to money, they must all stumble around in the dark the way everybody else must. Some are rich. Some are poor. Most are somewhere in between. Nearly all would like to be richer. In other words, they are no different from any group of men and women gathered at random anywhere.

Like most of the ministers, priests, and rabbis of the major religions, some occult gurus will tell you that they aren't in business to help you get rich. This is often a copout, but where it is genuinely meant, it is to their credit. Many gurus do promise help with money, however. So do most of the horoscopes you read in newspapers and magazines like *McCall's*. "Pisces: the period June 3-10 will be an auspicious time for investing. . . ."

If you ask the advocates of these mystical doctrines to show evidence that money can be made in this way, they will usually be able to do so. This is what makes the doctrines dangerously alluring. Like the prophets whom we studied under the Fourth Axiom, every occult practitioner can come up with at least one good story about a lucky hit. Some of the stories are astonishing indeed. If you have a friend or neighbor who is an occult believer, you may get an earful of this "evidence," and you may start to think *maybe, just maybe* . . . But hold tight to your skepticism and your money. The stories you will hear are all like Jesse Livermore's amazing adventure with Union Pacific. They don't prove that the given mystical approach is a great moneymaker. All they prove is that anybody who speculates long enough will sooner or later score a bull's-eye under seemingly weird circumstances.

I've had such experiences myself. The weirdest involved Tarot cards.

I became interested in the Tarot many years ago when a magazine asked me to write an article on the history of card games. It turned out that our modern fifty-two-card bridge and poker deck is a direct descendant of the seventy-eight-card Tarot deck. The Tarot was designed specifically for divination of the future, not for games, but something about it caught my attention. I became superficially proficient in giving Tarot readings. It was a good way to liven a dull party.

In the course of this research, inevitably, I heard money stories. The Tarot lends itself well to such stories, because many of its divinations deal directly with questions of wealth and poverty. One engaging story was told to me by officers of Godnick & Son, a leading Wall Street broker-dealer in puts and calls.

In case you aren't familiar with these wonderfully risky instruments, a call is a piece of paper that gives you the right to buy a stock at a fixed price over a future timespan. You buy a call when you believe a stock will rise in price. If it does, you make vastly more money by having a call on it than by owning the stock itself. If the price falls, on the other hand, you stand to lose your entire investment in a hurry. (A put, which doesn't directly concern us here, is the opposite: It gives you the right to sell a stock at a fixed price over a future timespan.)

A shabbily dressed man walked into Godnick's Beverly Hills office one day and said he wanted to buy some calls on Control Data. He had with him a check for slightly less than $5,000, drawn on a local savings bank and made out to himself. He had evidently just closed out a savings account. Godnick's California manager, Marty Tressler, deduced from various clues that this amount was virtually the man's entire net wealth. In view of that, Tressler asked some worried questions of the strange customer.

Was he sure he wanted to risk the whole amount? Tressler wanted to know. The man said yes, he was sure. All of it on one stock? Yep. But why Control Data, for Pete's sake? Control Data at the time was not attracting much attention around Wall Street. The company was felt to have a lot of bad problems that would take years to straighten out. The shares were trading around $30 when they traded at all, which wasn't often. The typical speculator's reaction to Control Data was to give it a quick glance and say, "Well, yeah, could be interesting one day. Maybe I'll look at it again next year."

But Marty Tressler's customer was perfectly sure Control Data was the vehicle he wanted. Tressler went on asking why. The man finally mumbled something about the Tarot.

He had received a hot tip from the cards. At the risk of driving him away, Tressler argued with him. But the man would not be shaken. He insisted on putting his entire wad into calls on Control Data. Tressler reluctantly took his $5,000 and wished him luck.

Six months later, because of factors that could not have been foreseen by any rational means, Control Data was one of the hottest stocks in creation. It was trading over $100. Tressler's odd customer came in and said he wanted to cash out of his call position. Tressler handed him a check for somewhat more than $60,000. The man had better than triple-quadrupled his money in half a year. He walked out into the street, and Godnick & Son never saw him again.

Amazing, right? But the story continues. Enter myself.

The story as I've told it thus far was related to me by Bert Godnick, the "& Son" of the firm, over dinner one night at a Wall Street watering spot. I listened with a special personal interest, for it happened I owned a few hundred shares of Control Data myself.

I hadn't been as prescient as Marty Tressler's Tarot-reading customer. I hadn't bought in at $30. Instead I'd come aboard at around $60, when excitement was building up about the company and I had a hunch it might build up higher. The hunch had proved correct. The price had continued to rise dramatically. On the day of my meeting with Godnick, it had leaped several points and landed just shy of my preplanned ending position, $120.

We talked about the Tarot and about Control Data. Godnick was not enthusiastic when I told him I planned to sell when the price hit $120. As a seasoned speculator he understood all about ending positions, but he believed this was a time when I should think about making an exception. His hunch was that the excitement could continue to build for several more months. Control Data could go a lot higher, he thought. We discussed this. He finally suggested jokingly that if I wasn't sure what to do, I ought to consult my Tarot deck.

For fun, I did just that the next day.

There are several ways to get "guidance" from a Tarot deck. One is to ask a specific question: "What should I do about such-and-such?" or "What are the prospects for this-and-that?" You then shuffle and lay out the cards in a prescribed way, and you study them. Information about your question is supposedly contained in the order in which various picture and suit cards turn up, and in whether they are right side up. (Unlike the cards in a modern playing deck, Tarot picture cards all have a top and bottom.)

I went through the drill with my question about Control Data's prospects. Tarot answers are usually equivocal, with a lot of "maybe . . . but on the other hand . . ." To my surprise, the answer I got this time had no maybe about it. It stood there flatfooted and said Control Data had a perfectly glorious future. I had never seen a Tarot layout so sure of what it wanted to say.

Frank Henry would have been ashamed of me. Never before in my life had I been swayed in financial affairs by a religious or occult persuasion. And only a very few times before or since have I ever reneged on a self-promise to get out of a game on reaching an ending position. But the Tarot had me hooked. The stock price reached $120, and instead of selling out I just sat and watched.

In my own defense I will say I didn't lean on the Tarot's prediction to the extent of getting lulled to sleep. I maintained a healthily worried state, ready to bail out at the first sign of trouble. But for weeks no such sign appeared. That crazy stock climbed straight uphill to $155.

By now I was really worried. When you pass an ending position without getting out, you feel as though there are giant rubber bands trying to pull you back. The farther away you run, the more taut they get. When the stock hit $155, I read the Tarot again.

This time the reading was appallingly bad. Violent change and ghastly misfortune lay ahead, the cards said. I immediately did what I'd wanted to do all along: sold out.

The stock struggled to $160, then plunged. For those still in the investment, it was a catastrophe. Wave after wave of sell orders pounded the price down, each wave triggering the one below it. When the panic ended about nine months later, the price was $28.

The Tarot had saved me!

But had it? I came to my senses eventually. There was no evidence whatever, in fact, that my good fortune had been brought about by any magical properties in the cards. All that had happened was that I had had a couple of strokes of good luck.

To depend on the same kind of luck under similar circumstances in the future—even to hope for it—would be foolhardy indeed. It could lead straight to my financial doom. Understanding this, I quickly backed away from the occult illusion of order that had almost had me in its soothing clutch. I put that Tarot deck away with a vow never to play with it again except for entertainment at parties. I kept the vow. In time even that casual use lost its appeal. My interest in the Tarot faded, and today I don't even know where that troublesome deck is.

If astrology worked, the minor axiom says, all astrologers would be rich. And so it is with Tarot devotees. Anybody can have a lucky hit or two, but the true test of any touted moneymaking approach is whether it works consistently. If I had any doubts that I was right to reject occult help after that Control Data adventure, those doubts were laid to rest once and for all a short time later.

I had lunch in New York one day with a self-styled Tarot master. The lunch was at his invitation. He was in the business of giving Tarot readings, and he also sold cards and an instruction book. Learning that I was thinking of writing more articles on the topic, he saw a chance to get some publicity. This was okay by me. He was an interesting fellow. He had assured me that the Tarot was one of the world's best ways to achieve one's financial goals.

After lunch the waiter came around with the check. The Tarot master acted as though he hadn't noticed it. I finally picked it up. He grinned and said, "We might as well put it on your expense account, right?" As a matter of fact I was not then operating under an expense authorization from anybody, but I let it go.

On the sidewalk outside, things got still more amusing. Explaining that he was having a "temporary cash-flow problem," the Tarot master bummed a fiver off me for cab fare.

I never saw him or my fiver again. But I didn't grieve for the money. I looked on it as an educational expense.

MINOR AXIOM XIII.
A superstition need not be exorcised. It can be enjoyed, provided it is kept in its place.

Most of us carry at least a few pieces of superstitious baggage about with us. Even if we aren't full-dress devotees of an occult belief such as astrology, we keep good-luck charms or have an aversion to the number 13. As we've seen, any religious, mystical, or superstitious belief can be a serious hazard to anybody who would get rich.

But if you do harbor such a belief or semibelief, you don't have to embark on a laborious program of scoffing it out of your life. Such a program would probably fail anyhow. If you don't like walking under ladders, you don't like it. Instead of exorcising it, all you have to do is learn how and when it can reasonably play a role in your financial life.

The role will be distinctly minor, even trivial. But if you are fond of this mystical or quasi-mystical thing of yours, at least you will be able to keep it as a pet.

In what follows I will be using the word "superstition" from time to time. I intend no sarcasm or disapproval in this usage. What's superstition to me may be religion to you, and vice versa. As used here, "superstition" means a supernatural belief that isn't shared by everybody.

There is a *way* to let a superstition into your financial life, and there is a *time* to do it. One of each: just one. All other ways and times can lead you to disaster.

The way to do it is humorously.

The time to do it is when you are in a situation that absolutely will not lend itself to rational analysis.

An example: picking a number to play in a state lottery or numbers game. One number is as good as another. There are no handholds for analysis. No amount of cogitation is going to give you even the most microscopic edge over other players. The outcome will be determined entirely by chance. We've noted that chance plays an enormous role in other money ventures such as the stock market, but at least there you have an opportunity to do some thinking and hunching in the struggle for speculative advantages. In the case of a pick-a-number game there is no such opportunity.

Then what do you do? There is only one thing you can do. Relax. Have some fun. With a grin on your face—for it is important never to take this kind of approach seriously—lean on your pet superstition.

Charles Kellner of Hillsdale, New Jersey, is a man who plays this fiddle perfectly. He has his money in real estate, a restaurant, and other ventures, and where those are concerned, no supernatural belief ever intrudes on his calculations. But when he plays the New Jersey state numbers game, he falls back on something that he cheerfully admits is weird: tips received in dreams.

In one New Jersey game you try to guess a three-digit number. Your ticket to play costs you 50 cents, and if you win, you get $500. Charlie Kellner had been playing this game without success for a time when, one night, he had a dream about a haunted house. The house number, 283, had some importance in the plot of the dream, and Charlie found this number lodged in his mind when he awoke. He does not know why. It was not a number that had any significance to him. Just for fun, however, he bet on 283 in the lottery that day—and lo and behold, won $500.

Not many weeks later he had another dream, this time about his mother. In the same spirit of fun, he bet the next day on the number of a house where she had once lived. That number, too, proved a winner.

"He's Charlie the Three-Digit Dreamer," says his wife, Dolores. "I'm going to load him up with sleeping pills. He makes more money per hour asleep than he ever did awake."

Charlie Kellner has fun with his nocturnal omens. They play only the most inconsequential part in his financial affairs. He lets them intrude only at times when he is playing games with his money and only in situations that are impervious to rational figuring-out.

Not being of a superstitious turn of mind, he doesn't believe he really possesses a magical ability to generate prophetic dreams. But even if he did—or even if he harbored a whispery little thought that it might be so—it would make no difference to his financial well-being. By using the superstition in the right way at the right time, he gets it out of his system.

Speculative Strategy

Now let's review the Eighth Axiom. What does it have to say about money and religion and the occult?

It says, essentially, that money and the supernatural are an explosive mixture that can blow up in your face. Keep the two worlds apart. There is no evidence that God has the slightest interest in your bank account; nor is there any evidence that any occult belief or practice has ever been able to produce consistently good financial results for its devotees. The most anybody has ever been able to show is an occasional, isolated bull's-eye hit, which gets a lot of attention but proves nothing except that lucky flukes happen.

To expect help from God or from occult or psychic powers is not just useless but also dangerous. It can lull you into an unworried state—which, as we've seen, is not a good state for a speculator to be in. In handling your money, assume you are entirely on your own. Lean on nothing but your own good wits.

The Ninth Major Axiom:
ON OPTIMISM AND PESSIMISM

Optimism means expecting the best, but confidence means knowing how you will handle the worst. Never make a move if you are merely optimistic.

Optimism has always had a good press. It is felt to be a nice trait to have. Optimistic people are cheerful souls, good company in gloomy times. During the Great Depression of the 1930s there was a nationwide network of Optimist Clubs, whose appealing doctrine was that things would get better if only people *believed* they were getting better. The Depression did go away after a while, and some optimists said, "See? It worked!" Perhaps optimism did play a role—with a helping hand from the Second World War. But you had better be very careful about the role optimism plays in your personal financial life.

A general feeling of hope and good expectations cannot do you any harm. "I'll learn. I'll do well. I'll make it." Indeed, without that fundamental buoyancy, how could one be a speculator at all? But be extremely wary of optimism as it applies to specific money ventures. It can be a dangerous state of mind.

Professional gamblers know this. It is one of their most effective tools for emptying the pockets of amateurs.

In poker, if a pro arrives at a situation in which the odds say he shouldn't bet, he doesn't. He folds. This means he must abandon what he has so far contributed to the pot, but it saves him from a bigger loss.

In the same situation, the amateur gets befuddled by optimism. "Maybe I'll be lucky," he thinks. "Maybe I'll draw my card. . . . Maybe the guy across the table is bluffing about that doughnut straight of his. . . ."

Once in a while, of course, the amateur does get lucky. What the odds said probably wouldn't happen does happen. The amateur beats the odds just often enough to keep that crazy optimism alive. And so he keeps investing his money in losing hands. You can beat the odds once in a while but not consistently. Usually, if the odds say you've got a loser, it's a loser. The pro, knowing this, and knowing how easily the optimistic sucker can be persuaded to bet when he shouldn't, gets rich.

The pro doesn't have optimism. What he has is confidence. Confidence springs from the constructive use of pessimism.

An optimist, descending into the valley of the shadow, puts on a brave smile and says, "Things never are as bad as they seem." Or instead of saying it, sings it. Almost as many songs have been written on that theme as on unrequited love. It is certainly a nice gooey theme, but don't ever let it get mixed up with your financial philosophy. In poker and a lot of other speculative worlds, things nearly always *are* as bad as they seem. A lot of times, they're worse. They are worse at least as often as they are better. You can bet on better if you like, but in the absence of tangible evidence to the contrary, you're being overoptimistic. The safest course, almost always, is to assume that if a situation looks bad, it is.

"Never make a move if you are merely optimistic," says the Axiom. Seek confidence instead. Confidence comes not from expecting the best, but from knowing how you will handle the worst.

The poker pro knows what he is going to do if the cards fall against him. Of course, he hopes they won't, but he doesn't let his fate ride on that hope. He goes into the game trained and prepared to act sensibly in case his luck of the draw is bad. That's what is meant by constructive pessimism.

In contrast, let's look at the sad saga of a young married couple who thought optimism was enough. We'll call them Sam and Judy—not their real names. Their story was told to me by a San Francisco–suburban real estate saleswoman.

Sam and Judy were fairly typical of the breed sometimes labeled yuppies—young urban professionals. Sam was an advertising man, Judy a pediatric resident in a hospital. They nursed big dreams. Sam wanted to found his own ad agency some day, while Judy planned to go into private practice. Possessing a healthy streak of acquisitiveness, they talked frankly of getting rich. To hasten that day, they had begun early in their married life to expose their spare money to risk.

They hadn't done too badly at first, considering their lack of skill as speculators. Luck had been with them. Over a span of several years they had managed to double their nest egg, which, when they married, had consisted of two savings accounts totaling about $12,000. They had parlayed it up to $25,000 or so. Then their luck ran out.

They learned about a vast land development in a southwestern state. Lots of various sizes from half an acre up were being offered as homesites or for investment purposes. The development corporation, however, had overextended itself. Roads had been built and utility lines extended into one area of the vast tract, as promised, but then the company had run out of money. Much of the tract was still nothing but an untouched wilderness of semidesert.

To raise the cash it desperately needed, the corporation had progressively dropped the price of lots in the unimproved part of the development. Outlying lots were being offered at prices that seemed astonishingly low when compared to prices in the improved segment.

Sam and Judy studied this interesting situation with a good deal of excitement. By using most of their nest egg, they could buy an impressively big acreage in that outlying area. By reselling lots when the time came, they could double or triple their money in a short time—*if*.

If these promised roads ever got built. And if those utility lines ever made their way to the outlying area.

It was a gamble on the fate of the development corporation. If the company regained its health, and if various legal questions were resolved in its favor, and if a number of other things, then, in time, roads and utilities would push their way out to the lots Sam and Judy were looking at. But if things went badly, those lots might be inaccessible wilderness forever.

The company's sales literature and salespeople made promises, of course—or to put it more accurately, mumbled encouraging phrases that sounded like promises but didn't legally bind the company to do anything: "It is anticipated . . . the directors believe . . ." Sam and Judy weren't naive enough to be taken in by this. They were aware of the risks. The corporation might go bankrupt. Or the shareowners might simply vote it out of existence, pick up the residual cash, and scatter like seeds in the wind. In such a case, Sam's and Judy's land would be worth even less than the bargain price they were paying for it. It might even turn out to be just plain unsalable. Their money could be trapped in it for the rest of their lives.

But they thought the risk was worth taking. They were optimistic.

There is nothing wrong with taking a risk, of course. To bet one's money on a venture whose outcome cannot be foreseen: this is the basis of all speculation. As we've learned in studying other Axioms, just about *all* ventures have unforeseeable outcomes. There are no reliable patterns in human affairs. No forecast can be trusted. Whether you're buying IBM stock or undeveloped land, you're still gambling. In putting their money at risk in hope of a gain, Sam and Judy weren't doing anything that isn't done daily by all those supposedly prudent Wall Street people who like to call themselves "investors."

But Sam and Judy made one fundamental mistake. They weren't pessimistic enough. They didn't ask how they would save themselves if the cards fell against them.

Buying IBM stock is a gamble, but there is a way to save yourself if the venture sours. You sell out. We noted under the Third Axiom that this isn't the easiest thing in the world to do, but at least the chance to do it is open to you. There is always going to be somebody to sell to, for there is always somebody making a market in IBM shares. Walking into the venture, you can mark the exit: "I'll get out if the price drops to such-and-such."

Knowing how you will handle the worst: that is confidence.

Sam and Judy could have made an exit for themselves if they had been less optimistic. The land they were looking at was more than a mile from the developed segment, where the paved roads ended. This distance was part of the reason for the extremely low price. Other undeveloped plots were also for sale, closer to the developed segment but at correspondingly higher prices. Sam and Judy could have bought some of this higher-priced land. Then, if the corporation failed to make good on its promises, they could have made their land usable and salable by putting in their own relatively short access road.

If they had to do that, they might come out of the venture with a loss. But at least they would be able to get out.

Instead of thinking about that gloomy possibility, they bet on their optimism alone. The situation seemed full of promise to them. If the development corporation recovered from its difficulties and carried out its announced plans, which Sam and Judy found every reason to believe it would, they and other holders of outlying plots stood to make an eye-popping gain. And so Sam and Judy walked into a venture with no exit.

That was many years ago. The corporation no longer exists. Nor do the promised roads and utility lines. The state attorney general's office has been trying to track down the company's principals and force an accounting from them, but with little success so far. Meanwhile Sam and Judy are stuck with a lot of land that can only be reached on foot or on horseback and seems likely to remain that way.

They may never sell it. They and other owners of outlying plots have talked about sharing the cost of access roads and utilities, but nothing ever gets done. The projected costs are high, and while some property owners seem willing to pay their share, others aren't. Sam and Judy, betrayed by optimism, are in what could be a life-long trap.

One reason why optimism is so treacherous is that it feels good. It feels much better than pessimism. It has a hypnotic allure. It is like the Sirens of ancient Greek legend, whose sweet singing lured sailors to death on the rocks.

Any venture, as you begin it, has a limitless number of possible futures, some good and some bad. The good ones and the bad ones are equally likely. You're as likely to go down as up. But which kind of outcome *feels* the more likely to you? The good kind, of course.

Optimism is altogether human and probably incurable. Peering blind-eyed into an impenetrable future, we hope for the best and talk ourselves into *expecting* the best. Perhaps life would be impossible without optimism. Speculation would be impossible too. The very act of betting money is a species of optimistic statement about an unknowable outcome. This is the paradox of it: optimism, which feels so good and may even be necessary, can lead to financial doom if allowed to get out of control.

Not only does it lead to Sam's and Judy's kind of doom, but it is a leading cause of pervasively flawed judgment. This is illustrated every business day on Wall Street. No matter what the stock market happens to be doing on any given day, there are always optimists around saying the next great bull market is going to start next week. There are also pessimists saying it isn't. Who gets listened to? Most often the optimists, for their song is the sweeter.

You can check this for yourself. Great financial newspapers such as the *Wall Street Journal* and the *New York Times* publish columns of stock market news, gossip, and opinion every day. The business journalists who write these columns hit the phone every afternoon when the markets have closed. Calls go out to brokers, analysts, and others who can be expected to comment knowledgeably on the day's trading. Each journalist has a list of favorite people who can be buttonholed for this purpose. On what basis does the journalist decide whom to call? What qualifies somebody for a position at the top of one of these lists? Mainly three things: accessibility, articulateness, and optimism.

By my own informal count over a period of years, at least three-fourths of the market readings reported in these columns are optimistic. This is a decidedly lopsided showing, since, from any given day's viewpoint, the market's future is just as likely to be bad as good. There should be pretty nearly an equal number of bears and bulls around. Yet if we are to go by the newspaper columns, bulls are vastly in the majority. Why? There are two explanations:

First, bulls do, in fact, outnumber bears—by a very big margin. The reason for this is, of course, that optimism feels better than pessimism. So even if a conscientious journalist were to beat the bushes for an equal number of quotable bears and bulls, with the object of writing a carefully balanced report, he would be frustrated by the fact that bulls are considerably easier to find.

Second, financial journalists don't usually seek equal bull-bear representation in any case. Why not? Because they prefer interviewing bulls. The song is sweeter. So even if there were an equal number of the two species wandering about on the Street, the bulls would still be overrepresented in the reports.

The more bullish of the bulls get quoted over and over again by everybody. There is one man whose name appears in the papers or on radio or TV business reports at least once every two weeks. He is an officer of one of the Street's biggest and oldest brokerage houses. He is such an amiable soul, and the song he sings is so beautiful, that I don't want to embarrass him or tarnish his image by naming him here. It would be sinful, one feels, to risk souring that music.

The journalists keep going back to him because he is such a diehard optimist. The fact that he is usually wrong doesn't seem to upset anybody or diminish his appeal. All through 1980 and 1981 he kept doggedly predicting that a bull market was about to start. It didn't, but the journalists kept quoting him. He finally became right in August 1982. The bull market arrived, then petered out in the spring of 1983. Never mind, said this cheerful soul, all we're seeing is a temporary pause in the bull market! He kept saying that the Dow Jones Industrial Index would soon top 1300. It didn't. By the first quarter of 1984 it was slumping toward 1100. But this only made the quotable fellow stoke up his optimism all the higher. All it took was one good day in the market to convince him that paradise was at hand. Early in April, after weeks and weeks of gloom, the Dow managed to jump some twenty points in one day's trading. The optimist was quoted in the *New York Times* as saying that this was the beginning of the second great leg of the bull market.

The next day, the Dow gave up about half of its twenty-point gain. The day after that, it gave up the rest.

The promised "second leg" seemed to be delayed a bit. But this didn't seem to perturb the optimist or diminish the number of journalists' calls coming in on his phone. A week or so later, he was singing his cheery song into the ear and typewriter of a *Wall Street Journal* reporter.

Thus does the exasperating human psyche operate. We are drawn to optimism and optimists. They plainly don't know any more about the future than pessimists do; nor can we ever assume, in choosing between the two, that the optimists are objectively more worth listening to. Yet, as you will learn if you haven't already, it is the optimists to whom you would prefer to lend your ear.

There are optimists all around you, and there is undoubtedly a very insistent one inside your head. Watch out for them all. They can befuddle your good judgment to an alarming degree.

In the old legend, Odysseus got his ship safely past the Sirens by plugging his crewmen's ears with wax and having himself roped to the mast. No such defense is effective against the song of the optimist. You will never block the song out entirely, for you are, after all, human. What you *can* do is to stay aware of the optimistic bias in your internal compass and stay alert to its dangers.

When you're feeling optimistic, try to judge whether that good feeling is really justified by the facts. At least half the time, it won't be.

Speculative Strategy

The Ninth Axiom warns that optimism can be a speculator's enemy. It feels good and is dangerous for that very reason. It produces a general clouding of judgment. It can lead you into ventures with no exits. And even when there is an exit, optimism can persuade you not to use it.

The Axiom says you should never make a move if you are merely optimistic. Before committing your money to a venture, ask how you will save yourself if things go wrong. Once you have that clearly worked out, you've got something better than optimism. You've got confidence.

The Tenth Major Axiom:
ON CONSENSUS

Disregard the majority opinion. It is probably wrong.

René Descartes was the world's champion doubter. He stubbornly refused to believe anything until he had verified it for himself. This was one of the traits that made him a successful gambler-speculator. He died more than 300 years ago, but any modern speculator can profit greatly—as well as spend a lot of enjoyable evenings—by reading the works of this engagingly ugly man with the staring black eyes, the nose like a crescent moon, and the giant intellect.

Descartes began his philosophy by doubting literally everything, including the existence of God, man, and himself. This enraged the religious authorities of his native France, so he fled to the Netherlands. Continuing to reject what others told him was true, he searched for ways of discovering truth through his own senses and experience. He finally hit upon what he considered a basic and unarguable truth: *Cogito, ergo sum*—"I think, therefore I am." Having thus satisfied himself that he wasn't just a phantom of his own dream, he went on to verify or reject other postulated truths. In the process he made major contributions to mathematics and built a philosophy which, for sheer lucidity of thought, hasn't been surpassed in three centuries. (For my money, there haven't even been any close competitors.) And also in the process, partly as a hobby and partly because he had a taste for costly wines and other luxuries, Descartes made a scientific study of gambling.

There were only a few loosely organized stock and commodity exchanges in existence in the first half of the seventeenth century. Descartes was fascinated by the big, lively market at Amsterdam, but whether he took any fliers there, and how big those fliers were, is not known. What is known is that he often traveled to Paris, sometimes under an assumed identity to avoid arrest for heresy, and gambled.

Various card, board, and spinning-wheel games were available, ready to take suckers' money. Descartes enjoyed games whose outcomes, like those of modern bridge or poker, depended not only on luck but also on mathematical computation and psychology. He studied his games with customary care and skepticism, rejecting all the gambling clichés and folk wisdom of the time, insisting on establishing truth or fallacy for himself. He seems always to have gone home from Paris richer than he arrived, sometimes a lot richer. Though his only visible means of support through most of his adult life was a small inheritance from his father, he died comfortably well off.

The trick, he said over and over again in any number of contexts, is to disregard what everybody tells you until you have thought it through for yourself. He doubted the truths alleged by self-styled experts, and he refused even to accept majority opinions. "Scarcely anything has been pronounced by one [learned person] the contrary of which has not been asserted by another," he wrote. "And it would avail nothing to count votes . . . for in the matter of a difficult question, it is more likely that the truth should have been discovered by few than by many."

It was with this perhaps arrogant and certainly lonesome view of the world that René Descartes went to the gaming tables of Paris and walked away rich. If you would succeed as a speculator, you could do a lot worse than to listen to the words of this hard, clear-eyed man.

In our democratic age, on our democratic side of the world, we tend often to accept majority opinions too uncritically. If a lot of people say something is so, why, all right, it's so. Thus does our thinking run. If you aren't sure about something, take a poll. The rightness of majorities is pounded into our heads in grade school. It is very nearly a religion in America and other western nations, particularly those such as France and Britain, with a long history of deciding public issues by popular vote. If 75 percent of the people believe something, it seems almost sacrilegious to ask, even in a whisper, "Hey, wait a minute, could they be wrong?"

Listen to Descartes. They could.

In America we decide who will govern us by voting. That is the only sane way to do it. At least it is the only way any of us would sit still for. We are trained from school years on to accept the will of the majority. We often grumble about this will—we can always be heard fussing and fuming when our candidate loses—but in the background, behind all the sound and fury, you can always hear the democratic leitmotif: "The people have spoken. You can't fool them. If this is what they want, it must be right."

This humble acceptance of the majority opinion spills into our financial lives. We listen not only to economists, bankers, brokers, advisers, and other experts, but also to majorities. This can cost us money, for as Descartes said, it is more likely that the truth has been found by few than by many.

The many may be right, but the odds are they aren't. Get out of the habit of assuming that any often-heard assertion is the truth. "High budget deficits will be the ruination of America," says nearly everybody. Is it true? Maybe, maybe not. Figure it out for yourself. Come to your own conclusion. "Interest rates and inflation will rise as the decade grows older." Oh yeah? Don't just swallow it. Examine it. Don't let the majority push you around.

In our studies of other Axioms we've looked at many things that are asserted by the majority. A bird in the hand is worth two in the bush. Build up a diversified portfolio. Only bet what you can afford to lose. And so on. All these pieces of supposedly wise advice are embedded in the popular consciousness. You need only bring up the subject of investment at any cocktail party or coffee circle to hear the ancient bromides repeated. And as each moss-grown old preachment is uttered, everybody within hearing will nod sagely: "Yes. Quite right! Excellent advice!"

The majority of people believe the ancient clichés to be unarguable truths. In the light of this, it may be instructive to note that the majority of people aren't rich.

MINOR AXIOM XIV.
Never follow speculative fads. Often, the best time to buy something is when nobody else wants it.

The pressure of majority opinion is especially troublesome when it comes to the questions of what to invest in and when to invest. This is when many an otherwise clever speculator lets himself or herself be pushed around, with unprofitable results.

Take the stock market as an example. When is the best time to buy a stock? When the price is low, of course. And when is the best time to sell it? Why, when the price is high, naturally. Kids learn this in seventh-grade economics, and even if nobody ever taught it to them, they would figure it out for themselves.

What they don't usually learn until adulthood is that this seemingly simple formula is amazingly difficult to put into practice. It is difficult, in large measure, because it requires the speculator to act against the pressure of popular opinion.

As a general rule, the price of a stock—or any other fluid-priced speculative entity—falls when substantial numbers of people come to believe it isn't worth buying. The more unappetizing they find it, the lower the price drops. Hence the great paradox that isn't taught in seventh grade: The time to buy is precisely when the majority of people are saying, "Don't!"

And the obverse is true when it comes time to sell. The price of a speculative entity rises when large numbers of buyers are clamoring for it. When everybody else is screaming, "Gimme!" you should be standing quietly on the other side of the counter saying, "Gladly."

Let's look at a specific example. The automobile industry fell into a quagmire of highly publicized troubles at the beginning of this decade. The troubles were severe and, as far as anybody could tell, intractable. All of Detroit stared into a future that looked like the pit of hell. There was talk about widespread bankruptcies of auto makers and suppliers. Plant after plant shut down. Thousands of workers found themselves out on the streets without paychecks. In a desperate effort to conserve operating cash, mighty GM halved its stock dividend from 1979 to 1981, and in the following year Ford paid no dividend at all.

The majority opinion—all the way from Detroit's union halls to the clubs and watering spots of Wall Street—was that the auto industry was in deep mud and wasn't going to climb out for a long, long time. Anybody who bought auto stocks ought to have his or her head examined, the majority said. The stocks, unwanted, sank to dismal lows. You could buy GM common shares in 1981 and 1982 for $34—as low as it had been in more than twenty years—and many pundits predicted it would go still lower. Ford's stock (adjusting for a 3-for-2 split in 1983) could be had in those bad years for $11.

As it turned out, anybody who ignored the majority view in

those years made out fine. GM Stock, buyable up to mid-1982 for $34 or so, zoomed to $80 in 1983. Ford more than quadrupled, from $11 to $46 and a fraction.

The industry's troubles had been shorter-lived than most people had thought possible. The speculators who made money out of the situation were those who disregarded what everybody else was saying and thought things through for themselves.

But it is notoriously hard to think "yes" when everybody around you is shouting "no!" Some speculators find this to be among their worst problems. Majorities are always dissuading them from carrying out good moves.

It happened to my wife during the auto-industry upheaval. A six-month CD of hers came due in early 1982. She had a hunch about Ford, which was then, as we've noted, deep in the mire. She liked Ford's cars, kept hearing other women praising them, and believed the weeping and teeth-gnashing from Detroit were caused partly by a seizure of self-pity and panic, which would soon go away. And so she talked to her broker about buying some Ford stock.

He laughed at her.

He was a man immersed to the ears in the majority opinion. He was able to document that opinion abundantly. Newspaper stories, analysts' reports, and of course the low stock price itself—all sang together in a mighty chorus: "Don't buy!"

So she didn't. This was unusual for her. In most situations she is quite capable of thinking her way independently to her own conclusions. But in this case the majority pressure was simply too intense to resist.

Majority pressure can not only dislodge a good hunch; it can even make us doubt ourselves when we *know* we're right. They used to demonstrate this in the psychology department at Princeton University.

The experiment was unkind but startlingly effective. Eight

or ten people would be assembled around a table. In the middle of the table were half a dozen pencils of assorted colors. All the pencils were precisely the same length except one. That one —we'll say the red one—was clearly shorter than all the others.

The people around the table would be asked to vote on the lengths of the pencils. The majority—everybody but one baffled person—would express a clearly wrong opinion, one that argued with the evidence of the eyes. They would say that the pencils were all the same length.

The majority were coached and were in on the hoax, of course. They were all ringers except one. The object was to see how that one person would react.

In about one-third of the runs, the nonringer would undergo a moral collapse and go along with the majority opinion. Against the evidence lying plainly in view, he or she would squirm, fidget, sigh, and finally say yes, okay, I guess the rest of you are right, those pencils are all the same length.

Arguing with a majority is enormously hard. It is hard even when the debate deals with factual matters that can be verified by looking or measuring. It is vastly harder when the debate deals with questions of opinion that can't be subjected to that kind of quick verification. Nearly all money-world questions are of the latter variety.

As far as I know, there is no mental muscle-building course that can strengthen your ability to withstand majority pressure. At dinner parties sometimes, I deliberately make myself a minority of one by expressing some dumb opinion that I know will start everybody else beating on me—"Nuclear war may be less horrid than those old-time wars where you got hacked with swords," or some such nonsense. Trying to defend oneself against an enraged majority in a case like that is certainly stimulating. But whether it would strengthen you for the next time you want to buy a mired Ford, I don't know.

Probably the best defense against majority pressure is the

simple awareness of its existence and coercive power. Novice speculators often seem to lack this awareness. A novice can be bulldozed by a majority without even realizing it's happening.

Thus, you will always find novices among the herds of people swept along by speculative fads. When gold is the Speculation of the Month—when everybody is talking about it, every financial columnist furiously writing about it—that is when newborn speculators typically plunge in and buy. It is also when the price of gold is likely to be unnaturally high, but it seems to take people a long time to understand that. Similarly, when small-capitalization high-tech companies are the hotsies of Wall Street—and when their share prices are sky-high—that is when the newborn line up to add their money to the pile that will one day go up in smoke.

The novice gets pushed around without feeling the push. He or she doesn't stop to ask: "Am I making this decision because it's smart or because a majority *says* it's smart?" That is a question Descartes would have asked. If he were to invest in gold or high-tech, he would have done so only for his own reasons, regardless of what the herd was doing or saying.

In your effort to resist the pressure of the herd, you will also be up against sales pressure from brokers and others who stand to profit from your speculative moves. These speculation-service people, seeking their commissions and fees, naturally tend to push whatever is hot at the moment—whatever happens to be tickling the public fancy, whatever is high-priced. If you are an active speculator, you are always going to be bombarded with ads, sales talks, and other blandishments to buy whatever the majority is buying.

It isn't that the speculation-service folks harbor a malicious wish to make you poor. On the contrary, they would rather see you rich—partly because that means potentially higher fees for them and partly because they're human like the rest of us: They prefer being smiled at. Still, like anybody selling anything, they must pay attention to what the public wants.

The public almost always wants gold during recessions, for example. The yellow metal is felt to be a lockbox of value in times when national economies, currencies, stock markets, and other money structures are developing cracks and springing leaks. During a dark time such as the early 1980s, the price of gold tends to jump because large numbers of people are buying it.

As we've discussed, that is exactly the time when you should be the most cautious about doing the same. But it is also the time when the selling pressure for gold reaches its peak. In the early 1980s, newspapers were full of ads offering gold bullion, coins, and medallions. Brokers touted the shares of gold-mining companies such as Homestake. Unit trusts specializing in gold-related investments sent out truckloads of prospectuses and brochures. Advisory services offered reports on gold and prophecies about it. If you wanted to put your money into gold or any investment linked to the metal, all you had to do was place a toll-free phone call to any of a dozen numbers, and a battery of happy operators would be waiting to take your order.

But by the end of 1983, when economic conditions were looking rosier and the price of gold was down, you had to hunt hard to find anybody who would sell you a gold medallion.

None of this means you should always automatically do what the majority isn't doing. It means only that you should stubbornly resist majority pressure instead of just drifting along with it. Study each situation for yourself, process it through your own good brain. The chances are you will find the majority wrong, but that doesn't happen always. If you determine that everybody else is right, then by all means march with the majority. The point is: Whatever you do, whether you bet with the herd or against, think it through independently first.

There are speculators who make a dogma out of betting automatically against the majority. They call themselves contrary thinkers or contrarians. Their philosophy is derived from the paradox we've been looking at: that often the best time to buy something is the time when it seems the least attractive. Thus you will find contrarians doggedly buying stocks in the black pit of a depression, buying gold on the sunny peak of a boom, buying this or that school of paintings when everybody else is using them for freezer wrap.

The trouble with contrarianism is that it starts with a good idea and then hardens it into a grandiose illusion of order. It is true that the best time to buy something may be when nobody else wants it. But to buy automatically and unthinkingly for that single reason—to buy solely because the entity is unwanted—seems almost as silly as to bet unthinkingly *with* the herd.

The herd isn't *always* wrong. If the market value of Trashworthy's art drops to 10 cents a square yard, that could be a good buying opportunity. On the other hand, perhaps the herd is right to shun these gummy expanses of oil paint. Maybe they will never be useful for anything but wrapping fish.

Almost everybody shunned Chrysler stock in the early years of the decade, and in my opinion quite rightly. If it was risky back then to put one's money into the low-priced GM or Ford shares, it was the craziest of gambles to buy Chrysler. The company had one foot in the grave. A bitterly debated loan from Uncle kept the gasping corporate wreck alive, but its long-term prognosis was bleak. The unwanted stock could be bought for three or four bucks a share through most of the period 1980–82. In making that unenthusiastic judgment about Chrysler, the herd was acknowledging an objective reality: The company's chances of making a comeback were worse than poor. Chrysler looked like a terminal case.

Today, of course, we can look back with the 20–20 vision of hindsight and see that the popular judgment was too pessimistic. Against all odds, Chrysler fought its way back to health. The stock was trading over $35 by the end of 1983. By buying it at its low a year and a half earlier, you could have tenfolded your money.

That still doesn't change the fact that the stock, as seen from the viewpoint of 1981, was a long, long shot. The majority of speculators, in shunning it, were acting in a perfectly reasonable way. Here was a case in which a contrarian's kind of bet, automatically against the majority, would have seemed pretty foolhardy.

Here was a case, indeed, in which it might have seemed sensible to make an exception to Minor Axiom i, which counsels that one should always play for meaningful stakes. A bet on Chrysler up to mid-1982 would have been like buying a lottery ticket or entering a raffle. Figuring that the odds are a million to one against you, you wager a couple of bucks just for fun. If Congress had passed a law in 1981 requiring every taxpayer to invest in Chrysler, I would have bought one share.

Well, maybe a hundred. It is nice to dream about tenfolding one's money in a year and a half.

Speculative Strategy

The Tenth Axiom teaches that a majority, though not always and automatically wrong, is more likely to be wrong than right. Guard against betting unthinkingly either with the majority or against, but particularly the former. Figure everything out for yourself before putting your money at risk.

The greatest pressures on you, and the most frequently felt, will be those that push you into betting *with* the majority. Such march-with-the-crowd speculations, the Axiom warns, can be costly, for it is in their nature that they tend to make you buy when prices are high and sell when they are low. The strongest line of resistance against these pressures is a keen awareness of their existence and insidious power.

The Eleventh Major Axiom:
ON STUBBORNNESS

If it doesn't pay off the first time,
forget it.

Perseverance is like optimism: It has always had a good press. "If at first you don't succeed, try, try again," an ancient English king is reported to have remarked, having watched a spider build a web after many bad starts. That is certainly good advice for spiders. Also for kings, who are usually born rich. For ordinary men and women like you and me, struggling to make a buck, it is advice that should be heeded selectively.

Perseverance can serve us well in many areas of life. You'll never get a straight answer out of the Motor Vehicle Department without it, for instance. In speculation, however, while there are times when it can be useful, there are also times when it can lead you to your financial doom.

How? A Merrill Lynch account executive told me a typical story.

Over a span of years ending recently, he said, he dealt with a woman customer who was obsessed with Sears, Roebuck. She was determined to make some money on the company's stock if she had to bankrupt herself in the attempt. She nearly did.

She had become fond of Sears while working at the University of Chicago in an administrative post. The company, whose corporate headquarters are in Chicago, has always been generous to the university. One fabulous gift was the Encyclopaedia Britannica publishing company, which Sears used to own but which since 1943, under various proprietorship and copyright arrangements, has poured much of its great river of income into the university's thirsty treasury. The woman of our story was charmed by this when she learned about it. She had determined back in her college days that if she ever became an investor, she would invest only in companies that seemed to be doing some substantial social good. Now that she was nearing age forty and at last had a little spare cash to play with, she decided that Sears was what she wanted.

There is nothing wrong with choosing investments on this kind of basis, as long as you don't forget that you're mainly in the market to make money. If you reject investments that for one reason or another offend your social or political sensibilities, that can narrow your field of choice somewhat but not necessarily badly. There are plenty of outfits like Sears, good corporate citizens that also make a bundle of money when things are going right.

The woman bought her first little packet of Sears stock. Unfortunately, the stock didn't repay her for her affectionate feelings. For reasons that nobody can ever sort out completely either before or after the event, customers chose the next twelve months to stay out of the stores and off the phones. The share prices of big retailers, including Sears, nosedived.

Acting on good advice—see the Third Axiom, on hope—she sold out, taking a 15 or 20 percent loss. The stock price continued to slump. She put her money in a bank.

The stock went nowhere for a year. Then, to everybody's surprise, it suddenly leaped. It shot past the point at which the woman had sold it and continued to climb.

She watched, baffled and angry. The higher the price went, the madder she got. She had the left-behind blues and had them bad. How *dare* the stock run away from her like that?

The stock owed her, she felt. She made up her mind that she was going to squeeze some money out of it if she had to wring its neck.

Perseverance was setting in. She called her broker and said she wanted to buy back into Sears. He argued with her. The price was pretty high, he felt. It was so high that the stock's yield (the yearly dividend payout expressed as a percentage of the price) was below 4 percent, which was historically unusual for Sears. But she stubbornly insisted. She wanted to get back into Sears and make it pay her what it owed her.

It didn't. It slumped again.

And so it went for years. Her determination to wring a gain out of that one investment blinded her to other opportunities, other good moves that she might have made. She "chased" Sears (as speculators call this kind of behavior), chased it over the tops of bull markets and down into the depths of bear markets, nearly always losing money because this obsession clouded her judgment and fogged her vision.

Finally, in late 1982, she had the satisfaction of owning Sears shares when they turned in a winning performance. That seemed to get the fixation out of her system. Sears stock had at last paid its debt to her, she felt.

But had it really? In all the years when she was chasing Sears, her money could have been in other ventures—ventures that were coolly chosen on their merits rather than out of sheer stubbornness. Some of those ventures might have made her rich. The Sears chase had left her only slightly better off than when she had started—and there had been times when, because of her refusal to abandon it, it could have made her a heavy loser. Only by blind luck had she come out a little bit ahead.

Is that any way to run a speculative program? No, but it is typical of new speculators. Even more seasoned speculators will sometimes chase an investment out of sheer cussedness, determined to squeeze some juice out of it at all costs. For reasons that I never clearly understood, Frank Henry kept buying in and out of real estate in the vicinity of Morristown, New Jersey, when he really ought to have had his attention elsewhere. He had lost money on a real estate venture there, and he was *damned* if he was going to sit still for it. I had the same kind of thing about IBM stock at one time and have only partially cured myself. The doggone stock owes me money, and though I don't trade in it anymore, I do keep imagining myself buying IBM puts or calls and getting irritated when they rise without me.

It's human but silly. How can an investment medium "owe" you money? A person can owe you. If that person fails to pay up, you have a right to dun him or her for the money and to get upset if the irresponsible behavior continues. But if you lose money on a precious metal or a work of art, it is illogical to personify the investment medium with thoughts about "owing." Not only is it illogical, but it can lead you into the chasing kind of behavior that is likely to cost you still more money.

You lose some money on Sears stock, let's say. Of course you want to gain the money back. *But why does the gain have to come from Sears?*

A given gain will be the same whether it comes from Sears or any other investment. No matter where you win it, it's still money. With a whole wide, wonderful world of possible ventures to choose from, what is the point of getting obsessed with the single investment in which you had a loss? Why persevere with Sears at a time when other investments, coolly considered, may look more promising?

The reasons for persevering are emotional and not easy to sort out. The thoughts about owing come from personification of the speculative entity, as we've noted. "This investment took money from me, and by God I'm going to haunt it until it pays me back!" Mixed with this are vague feelings about vengeance. "I'll teach that stock to make a fool out of me!" Then there is the wish to have one's judgment vindicated, which we looked at under another Axiom. "I'll be proved right in the end." All these emotional responses, seething and bubbling together, produce a state of mind in which the speculator's thinking goes haywire.

Rising above this emotional turmoil is no easier than a lot of other internal adjustments a speculator must make, but you've got to do it. As I remarked before when we were studying another difficult mental maneuver, this isn't a book of psychological counseling, and I have no tidy little shrinkish thoughts to offer. If you have trouble getting over an urge to persevere in a losing venture, maybe a talk with a friend, spouse, or bartender will help. Or it might clear your head to go to a good movie or concert and forget your troubles for a few hours. A four-mile walk does wonders for me. Each of us finds his or her own route to salvation.

Somehow or other, you must defeat the wish to persevere when perseverance will lead you astray. The ancient king's apothegm, as applied to speculation, needs to be quite thoroughly revised. If at first you don't succeed, the hell with it.

MINOR AXIOM XV.
Never try to save a bad investment by "averaging down."

The technique known as "averaging down" or "averaging losses" is one of the investment world's most alluring traps. It is like those fail-safe, surefire, double-guaranteed systems for beating a roulette wheel, which are hawked in the streets and bars of Las Vegas and Atlantic City. When you first examine such a system it seems unassailably logical. "Why, yes, this really would work, wouldn't it?" you say, wide-eyed with wonder. The loss-averaging technique is like the roulette systems, too, in that it will work sometimes—when the player is lucky. That, of course, adds to its allure. But you must be careful not to let it beguile you. It is a rose with poisonous thorns.

Here's how it is supposed to work. You buy 100 shares of Hoo Boy Computer at $100 a share. Your cost (ignoring brokerage commissions for the sake of simplicity) is $10,000. Things go badly, and the price plunges to $50. You seem to have lost half your investment. Alas! you weep. But wait! All is not down the tubes! Your friend and neighbor, Numbsley Skullbone, who never made a dime speculating in his whole life but knows every investment cliché by heart, counsels you to improve the situation by averaging down.

What you should do, Skullbone says, is buy 100 more shares of this dog at the new bargain price, $50. You will then own 200 shares. Your total investment will have been $15,000. Your average cost per share, therefore, will have dropped from $100 to $75.

Magic! By taking Numbsley Skullbone's advice, you can make a bad situation look less bad. By throwing in new money, you can make the old money look smarter!

Once you've averaged down in this way, Skullbone tells you, you won't have to wait so long to get out even. You don't have to wait till the trading price climbs back up to $100. All you have to wait for under the new circumstances is $75.

Beautiful, right?

Not exactly. All you do when you average down is to fool yourself. No matter how you squirm and wiggle, you are not going to change the fact that you *did* pay $100 for those original 100 shares. Buying 100 more at $50 doesn't change that fact. Talking about the new average price of $75 may make you feel better for a while, but it doesn't do a bit of good for your financial condition.

What the whole misguided operation may do to your financial condition, in fact, is to make it a lot worse. Hoo Boy Computer's stock price has plummeted from $100 to $50. Presumably the market has some reasons for this sharp diminishment in its estimation of the company. What are those reasons? Study them. Maybe they are valid. Maybe Hoo Boy faces a lot of years in which its earnings are going to be poor. Maybe the stock is a good investment to stay away from for the time being. If that is so, why on earth are you buying more of it?

In any situation where you are tempted to average down your costs, ask yourself this: "Would I buy Hoo Boy at $50 if I didn't already own a bundle I'd bought at $100? Is Hoo Boy an investment I'd choose today on its merits alone?" If the answer is no, don't throw any new money into the soured venture.

You might determine, of course, that the answer is yes. As the Tenth Axiom says, it is often profitable to bet against a majority. Perhaps your independent calculations will convince you that Hoo Boy's troubles won't last as long as most people expect, and that the $50 price level, therefore, is a genuine bargain-basement opportunity. It can happen.

But be very sure this isn't just wishful thinking. If you are hunting bargains, the stock market and all other speculative worlds are always full of them. Before you throw that $5,000 into your second round lot of Hoo Boy, ask yourself: "Why into *this* particular investment? Of all the potential bargains around, does this one really look the most promising to me? Or am I just trying to make myself feel better by averaging down costs?"

Like perseverance in general, of which it is a special type, cost-averaging clouds one's judgment. Determined to pull your Hoo Boy investment out of the soup, you concentrate on Hoo Boy to the exclusion of other speculations that might be far better.

You've lost money on Hoo Boy and want to gain it back. But as we asked before in connection with Sears, why does the gain have to come from Hoo Boy? It'll be the same good, spendable cash no matter where it comes from. Rid yourself of the Hoo Boy obsession and you vastly widen your field of choices and improve the chances of getting the gain you seek.

Another problem with this down-averaging dance is that it encourages you to disregard the important Third Axiom, on hope: When the ship starts to sink, don't pray. Jump.

As we noted in our studies of that Axiom, the decision to take a small loss and take it fast is never easy and can sometimes be acutely painful. One looks for excuses not to do it, and one dandy excuse is the thought that one is going to make everything turn out right by averaging down. "Oh, I don't have to sell out of this speculation now. I don't have to do *anything* now. If it sags a whole lot farther, I'll just buy a bunch more and average down. . . ."

So you sit there on the deck of the sinking ship, bravely refusing to move as the waters rise around you. Does it make sense? No, but you wanted an excuse for inaction, and that is what you've got. At a fear-filled time like this, it isn't to be expected that you will examine your excuse to see if it is logical.

Frank Henry knew a man who actually managed to talk himself into being *happy* when his speculations slumped. If he bought something and the price fell, he would buy more and average down his cost. The lower the price went, the more he would buy and the lower his average cost would fall and the happier he would become. This was one fancy psychological trick, but it kept him content. It didn't make him rich, however. He got stuck in some bad investments for years, continually averaging down and genuinely believing he was being smart.

Speculative Strategy

Now a quick review of the Eleventh Axiom. What does it counsel you to do with your money?

It says that perseverance is a good idea for spiders and kings but not always for speculators. Certainly you can persevere in your general effort to learn, improve, and grow rich. But don't fall into the trap of persevering in an attempt to squeeze a gain out of any single speculative entity.

Don't chase an investment in a spirit of stubbornness. Reject any thought that a given investment "owes" you something. And don't buy the alluring but fallacious idea that you can improve a bad situation by averaging down.

Value the freedom to choose investments on their merits alone. Don't give that freedom away by getting obsessed with one soured venture.

The Twelfth Major Axiom:
ON PLANNING

Long-range plans engender the dangerous belief that the future is under control. It is important never to take your own long-range plans, or other people's, seriously.

George and Martha met and married in the 1940s. George was an accountant. He had a job with a small CA firm. Martha was a secretary in an insurance agency. As was customary in those days, she left her job shortly after the wedding to concentrate on wifehood and motherhood. George's salary wasn't much, but it was steady, and so was he. The world seemed secure and cozy. To make it more so, at the suggestion of Martha's father, a small businessman, the young couple sat down with a financial counselor and constructed a Long-Range Plan.

This was considered a prudent, sensible, and altogether admirable thing to do, and still is. Every young couple ought to have a plan, all the sages said. People with plans and those without were felt to differ in the same way as the ant and the grasshopper in Aesop's fable. The dour and practical ant works all summer long in anticipation of the winter ahead, while the planless grasshopper just sits around singing in the sun. In the end, of course, the poor old grasshopper has to come around, hat in hand, to beg for food, while the ant has the satisfaction of saying, "Ha, ha, I told you so."

In real life, however, it is more often the ant who gets himself fumigated or has his nest torn up by a bulldozer. That's what comes of having roots (see the Sixth Axiom), and roots come partly from long-range plans. The grasshopper, lighter on his feet, just hops out of the way.

George and Martha today are a retired couple in their sixties. They are nearly broke. They will be entirely broke, busted flat and dependent on charity, if they live much longer. Hardly any element of their long-range plan has turned out the way it was supposed to.

They figured in the 1940s that they would like to retire on combined pension and Social Security income of $700 a month, or $8,400 a year. That was a whopping good income in the 1940s. As a matter of fact, in most questionnaires and tabulations of income, the very top bracket was usually "$7,500 and over." That was the peak of affluence. Nobody knew anybody who earned more.

Today, of course, $700 a month will rent you a small apartment—as long as you don't want to eat. If you insist on eating and also want money for clothes, medical bills, and other necessities, then you're in trouble.

George and Martha's long-range plan envisioned their buying a small house to retire into. They were going to buy it with spot cash so that they would have no monthly mortgage payments to worry about. To this end, the plan called for them to save some $20,000 by age sixty-five.

If you had $20,000 in the 1940s, you could buy two houses and have some change left over for a car. The plan didn't foresee that in the 1980s, that seemingly big amount of money would hardly buy a dog kennel.

George and Martha don't have the twenty grand in any case. During their passage to poverty they have been hit by some unexpected expenses (as everybody is) and misfortunes (as ditto). In the 1960s, George's employer got tangled into a messy dispute involving falsified corporate financial records, and the

CA firm turned belly-up. George's job vanished, and his planned-for pension went with it. He found another job after a long hunt, but he never did achieve the $700-a-month retirement income he and Martha had planned on. Since retiring they have had to draw on their savings. Though their money earns interest at three times the rate they foresaw (2 to 3 percent was usual in the 1940s), their principal is dwindling fast.

They live in a seedy little apartment, eat a lot of canned beans, and spend a good deal of time wondering what happened.

Two things happened: planning, followed by the unexpected.

George and Martha depended on their plan too much. They got themselves rooted in it. There were several times in George's undistinguished career when he could have jumped off in some promising new direction. He could have gone into business with a friend, for example. The friend wanted to start a CA practice of his own. Both practice and friend are now prosperous. At the time this opportunity was offered to George, however, it scared him. It seemed too risky. He and Martha retreated into the cozy comfort of their plan. They didn't *need* to take any risks, they figured. They had life all figured out. The plan assured them of a nice little house and a comfortable income in their old age. With that bird in the hand, why did they need to go for two in the bush?

Thus did they allow themselves to be hoodwinked by their own long-range plan. It didn't occur to them that the bird they thought they had in hand was going to fly away.

As the Axiom says, long-range plans engender a belief that the future is under control. This is a hair-raisingly dangerous belief.

Peering ahead, I can dimly see the structure of next week. There is just enough continuity in events to allow me to do that.

I can sit here on a Wednesday and make some kind of financial plan for next Wednesday, perhaps. Allowing a margin for error, I can make a fairly reliable prediction of the week-ahead value of my wife's and my stocks, real estate, bank accounts, silver, and other assets. Even this plan and prediction can be ridiculously wrong, of course. The stock market may collapse before next Wednesday, for all I know. I may run over somebody's toe with my car and get sued for every nickel I've got. Still, I feel fairly comfortable planning seven days ahead. The visibility isn't great, but it's tolerable.

A month ahead, the visibility dims markedly. A year ahead, it is fogged almost to opacity. Ten years . . . twenty years . . . that far ahead, there is no visibility at all. You can't even see vague forms or outlines. You can't see *anything*. It is like peering into a pea-soup fog in the dead of night. Whatever is waiting for us out there is entirely unknowable.

If you can't know what you're planning for, how can you construct a sensible plan?

To plan for a future one cannot see—this seems like an egregiously silly undertaking. Yet life-insurance salesmen, investment counselors, and other experts go on urging it, and families—particularly young families—go on doing it. Having a long-range plan is felt to be as laudable today as it was when George and Martha were starting out. And it will do you just about as much good.

A plan is a lifelong illusion of order. Economists, financial advisers, and others who sell twenty-year plans always talk as though the money world is an orderly place that undergoes change very slowly and predictably, like a tree growing. Peering into the next century, they see a financial world that will be basically like this one, only more so. It will be bigger, more automated, more this, more that. They arrive at these reassuring conclusions by observing trends that characterize our world today and extending those trends into the future. All very tidy, and it allows for concoction of a lot of long-range plans.

What all these hopeful planners either fail to recognize or choose to ignore is that the money world is only in a limited sense like a tree growing. It is ridiculous to think you can see the world's future simply by looking at trends in evidence today. Some of those trends will undoubtedly peter out or reverse themselves in the next twenty years. Nobody knows which ones. Whole new trends will spring into existence, factors that nobody today even dreams of. Unknowable events will take us by surprise. Booms and busts, upheavals, wars, crashes and collapses: who knows what we have ahead of us?

The world in which your financial affairs will be conducted twenty years hence is hidden behind a curtain through which no chink of light shows. You cannot even know if there will be a money world at all, or a dollar, or anything to spend the dollar on.

That being so, don't try to make long-range plans or allow other people to make them for you. They will only get in your way. Instead, stay light on your feet, like the grasshopper. Instead of attempting to organize your affairs to accommodate unknowable events in the future, react to events as they unfold in the present. When you see opportunities, go for them. When you see danger, jump out of the way.

The only long-range plan you need, as far as money is concerned, is an intention to get rich. Exactly *how* you will accomplish that purpose is something you cannot know except in the most general way. I'm fond of the stock market and am usually invested up to the ears in it, so I assume my personal *how* will have something to do with that particular speculative world. But that is all I know about my financial future and all I will ever attempt to know about it. The only kind of preparation I can make for the next century, therefore, is to continue studying the market, to go on learning and improving. If you can call anything so vague a plan, then that's it—that's my plan.

Yours should be similarly free-floating. Resolve to learn all you can learn about the kinds of speculation that attract you, but don't ever lose sight of the probability—no, let's say the certainty—that your speculative media and the circumstances affecting them are going to change in ways you cannot now imagine. Don't let a plan immobilize you. Don't get stuck, don't get rooted like the ant, a potential victim for fate's bulldozer.

MINOR AXIOM XVI.
Shun long-term investments.

An executive of the Swiss Bank Corporation, Frank Henry's alma mater, told me the sad story of a long-term investor named Paula W. (a pseudonym) who got herself bulldozed pretty thoroughly.

She had started adult life as a production-line worker at the Ford Motor Company. Taking advantage of the company's generous educational and self-improvement programs for employees, she had worked her way up to management. Along the way she had accumulated a few thousand shares of Ford common stock. Her husband died when she was in her middle fifties, leaving her as the owner of a big house in a Detroit suburb and a Florida holiday cottage, neither of which she wanted to maintain any longer. She decided to sell them both, take early retirement from Ford, put all the money into Ford stock, and live happily ever after on the dividends.

This was in the late 1970s. Ford was then paying a dividend of $2.60 a share. Putting the newly purchased stock together with her previous accumulation, she had something like 20,000 shares. The dividends thrown off by these shares totaled some $52,000 a year. This amount was fully taxable as income (except for the none-too-generous exclusion of $100 that our kindly IRS allows), but when supplemented by her small early-retirement pension, it made Paula secure and comfortable.

Her broker, also a woman, phoned her once or twice to warn that trouble seemed to be brewing in the auto industry. It might be a good idea to sell Ford before the price dropped, the broker suggested. If Paula was interested mainly in income, why didn't she consider buying shares of a big utility? Utility companies traditionally pay out a big percentage of their income in cash dividends. The stocks tend to move sluggishly in price, but the dividend yields are commonly in the range of 9 to 15 percent—a good two or three times what most other companies pay out.

But Paula said no, she would prefer to stick with Ford. She knew the company, trusted it, and felt comfortable with it. As for the possibility of a drop in the stock price, she said, that didn't concern her at all. It was a long-term investment. She had no plans to sell it in the foreseeable future. She didn't even check the stock price in a newspaper more than once a year or so. Up an eighth, down an eighth—who needed that kind of aggravation? She was above it. All she wanted out of her stock was one of those nice fat dividend checks every quarter. Beyond that, she told the broker, she just wanted her stock locked away in a vault and forgotten.

In 1980, Ford chopped its dividend from $2.60 per share per year to $1.73. Paula's income was down to $34,600.

As we noted before in another context, the auto industry's troubles were deepening in 1980, and all the big carmakers' stocks were plunging in price, including Ford's. Paula should have been out of it long before, but she was rooted.

In 1981, Ford cut its dividend to 80 cents. Paula's income dropped to $16,000.

In 1982, Ford paid no dividend at all. Paula was desperate by now. She had to sell some 4,000 shares during this bleak year to raise cash for living expenses and pay off some mounting debts. The stock price, of course, was appallingly low by this time. She was forced to sell those shares for far less than she had paid for them.

In 1983, Ford began to struggle out of the soup. The directors declared a 50-cent dividend. Paula had only 16,000 shares left at the beginning of the year, and during the year she had to sell off another 2,000 shares. Her dividend income in 1983 was in the neighborhood of $7,000.

Things looked a bit brighter in 1984. The dividend payout was $1.20. Paula, with 14,000 shares left, collected $16,000. It kept her alive, but it wasn't what she had envisioned in her long-range plan.

Jesse Livermore wrote: "I believe it is a safe bet that the money lost by [short-term] speculation is small compared with the gigantic sums lost by so-called investors who have let their investments ride. From my viewpoint, the [long-term] investors are the big gamblers. They make a bet, stay with it, and if it goes wrong, they can lose it all. The intelligent speculator will . . . by acting promptly, hold his losses to a minimum."

As we've seen, Livermore was not a 100 percent successful speculator. He not only made four fortunes but turned around and lost them, and finally he lost his life in some personal darkness. But when he had his speculative engine well oiled and tuned, it hummed like a Rolls-Royce. He was worth listening to.

So heed that central sentence of his: "The [long-term] investors are the big gamblers."

They surely are. Betting on tomorrow is chancy enough. Betting on a day twenty or thirty years in the future is absolutely crazy.

Long-term investment, like so many of the fallacious procedures we've looked at, does have its charms. The main one is that it relieves you of the need to make frequent, perhaps painful decisions. You make just one decision—"I'll buy this and sit on it"—and then relax. This caters to laziness and cowardice, two traits with which all of us are abundantly supplied. Moreover, having a long-term nest egg, coupled as most nest eggs are with some kind of a long-range plan, gives you that cozy immersed feeling. Life is all figured out! No thing of the night can get you! Or so you think.

Still another charm of many long-term investments is that they save on brokerage commissions. The more frequently you jump in and out of brokered entities such as stocks, currencies, or real estate, the more your capital is going to get chipped at by commissions and fees. This may have some importance in real estate, where commissions are large, but in most other speculative worlds it usually has scarcely more significance than a gnat bite. Still, many long-term investors use the commissions-and-fees question as a rationalization.

Your broker or dealer would prefer that you be a light-on-the feet, fast-moving kind of speculator rather than a long-term sitter. The more moves you make, the more money the broker/dealer makes. In this particular case, his financial interests coincide perfectly with your own.

Don't get rooted. Every investment should be, at the very least, reevaluated and made to justify itself afresh every three months or so. Keep asking yourself: Would I put my money into this if it were presented to me for the first time today? Is it progressing toward the ending position I envisioned?

This doesn't mean you have to keep jumping around just for the sake of jumping. But if circumstances have changed since you first got into this investment, if it is sagging, if that ending position seems to be receding instead of getting closer, if you see another opportunity that looks clearly more promising to you in the light of the changed conditions—then make a move.

The urge to sit on long-term nest eggs doesn't spring solely from our own laziness, cowardice, and other inward problems. There is also a good deal of sales pressure applied by the world around us.

Many big, publicly held companies, for instance, offer attractive-sounding arrangements by which employees can invest regularly in their own stock. You sign up to invest so much a month, and to make it easier for you, some companies will even arrange to deduct the amount from your paycheck and buy stock automatically. You never see the money. It's painless investment!

Or so they like to tell you. What this kind of arrangement does is to root you in a place where, perhaps, you may not always want to be rooted. What would have been the sense, for example, of getting stuck in a long-term investment in GM stock over the past couple of decades? The stock was trading above $90 in 1971. It hasn't been close since.

Individual brokers and dealers in various speculative entities also offer what they usually call "convenient" monthly investment plans. You kick in so much a month to buy whatever you specify. This doesn't inexorably lock you into long-term investments, but it does have that tendency. The danger of it is that it encourages you to concoct a long-range plan: "Let's see, now, if I invest X dollars a month in Hey Wow Electronics, and if the stock price rises by a modest 10 percent a year—why, by age sixty-five I'll have X thousand bucks! I'll be rich!"

Don't you count on it, my friend.

Unit trust salespeople will also wave a lot of alluring long-term blandishments before your dazzled eyes. Trust people, too, have their convenient monthly investment plans. They will send you charts in four scrumptious colors showing how nifty it would have been for you if you'd stuck with them over the past twenty years. Or if their performance was so miserable that no amount of clever charting can cover it up, then they will send you charts showing how terrific the future is going to be if you sign on.

Then there is the life-insurance industry. This is a world of appalling complexity. To boil it down to its essentials, however, we can say there are two main kinds of life insurance: those that root you in a long-term investment and those that don't. My advice: Shun the former.

Long-term investment life, which is sometimes called "whole" life but also goes by dozens of other names, is designed to do two things. It provides money for your beneficiaries in case you cash out, and it provides an annuity or cash lump for you in case you stay in the game beyond some stated age. In all its bewildering variety of forms, one thing doesn't change: It is very expensive.

The affable, conservatively dressed salesman who spreads his charts out on your coffee table, talking in reverent tones about long-range plans, sincerely wants you to buy this kind of life insurance. He will bank a walloping good commission if you come aboard. He wants you to commit your good money for twenty or thirty years, but the deal is probably less long-term for him than it is for you. In all likelihood it's front-end-loaded, meaning that he collects a good proportion of those thirty years' commissions in the first year or two.

His main selling point will be that you aren't *buying*, you're *investing*. If everything turns out right, eventually you'll get back what you put in, or a substantial part of it. Meantime your family will be protected in case you turn up your toes sooner than planned. Wonderful, no?

No. What the salesman is asking you to do is plain crazy. He wants you to make a commitment to invest thousands of dollars over a span of years into a far, far future. How do you know what the world will be like in that future? Sitting here today, how can you be sure you'll want to invest in this annuity setup ten years from now, or twenty? Maybe, indeed, the world will change in unforeseen ways and make that annuity worthless. So why lock yourself into it?

If you have dependents who would be in financial trouble without you, protect them by buying the cheapest term insurance. This will pay off on your death, but that is its only purpose. It locks you into nothing. If a time comes when your dependents don't need you anymore, or some other change happens in your life, you simply drop the insurance and stop paying the premiums. Meanwhile, because the premiums are low, you have had money to invest in ventures other than insurance.

All you can know about the future is that it will get here when it gets here. You cannot see its shape, but at least you can prepare yourself to react to its opportunities and hazards. There is no sense in just standing there and letting it roll over you.

Speculative Strategy

The Twelfth and final Axiom warns about the futility and the dangers of planning for a future one cannot see. Do not get rooted in long-range plans or long-term investments. Instead, react to events as they unfold in the present. Put your money into ventures as they present themselves and withdraw it from hazards as they loom up. Value the freedom of movement that will allow you to do this. Don't ever sign that freedom away.

The Twelfth Axiom says there is only one long-range financial plan you need, and that is the intention to get rich. The *how* is not knowable or plannable. All you need to know is that you will do it somehow.